Meditations
on the
Sunday Gospels

Meditations on the Sunday Gospels

Year B

compiled and edited by
John E. Rotelle, O.S.A.

New City Press

Published in the United States by New City Press
202 Cardinal Rd., Hyde Park, NY 12538
©1996 Augustinian Heritage Institute

Cover art: Ave Center, Loppiano, Italy
Cover designed by Nick Cianfarani

Library of Congress Cataloging-in-Publication Data:

  Meditations on the Sunday Gospels / introduced and edited by John E.
  Rotelle.

    Includes bibliographical references and index.
    Contents: [1] Year B.
    ISBN 1-56548-082-1 (v. 2 : pbk.)
    1. Church year meditations. 2. Bible. N.T. Gospels
  —Meditations. 3. Catholic Church—Prayer-books and devotions
  —English.   I. Rotelle, John E.
  BX2170.C55M43   1995
  242'.3—dc20   95-9013

Printed in the United States of America

Contents

Foreword

From the earliest days of Christianity there has always been an emphasis on reading. The New Testament was written so that people would be able to reflect on it; from century to century it was copied and brought to other parts of the world. The writings of the Greek, Latin, Syriac, and other Church writers were also copied and transported from monastery to monastery, from city to city, from country to country. All this was done so that people would have access to the wisdom and insights of these Church writers.

With an anthology of readings you do much the same thing. You take the best of Church writers over the centuries and present these excellent and timely writings to posterity.

In this present collection of readings I selected those readings which best accompany the gospel passage for each Sunday of the three-year cycle of gospel readings and which convey some kind of message for our day and age. The reading is aligned with each gospel passage which is given in summary form at the very beginning. At times the gospel passage has one theme; where there are several themes in the gospel passage, a choice of one theme or other has to be made. The reading is not a commentary, in the strict sense, on the gospel; the reading was selected as a reflection, meditation, or elongation of the gospel.

I purposely stayed within the framework of what historians call the modern era—seventeenth to the twentieth centuries. At times I did select, by way of exception, some readings from earlier centuries. My reason for staying within this framework is twofold: First, I wanted to emphasize the importance of the modern era and that tradition is ongoing and does not just stop with the Fathers of the Church; secondly, I respected what has already been published, for example, *Journey with the Fathers,*[1] which is along the

---

1. E. Barnecut, ed., *Journey with the Fathers*, Year A, B, C (Hyde Park: New City Press, 1992-94).

lines of this book with a heavy emphasis on Church writers, and *Tradition Day by Day*,[2] readings for each day of the year from Church writers.

Lectio Divina

When we hear the word "reading," we immediately think of taking up a newspaper, magazine, or book and reading through it for information or for enjoyment. This is one type of reading. However, there is another type of reading in the Church's tradition, in which one reads not for information, although this may come with the reading, nor for enjoyment, although this can be present, but for the enrichment of the inner spirit. It is a type of reading that is a prayer in itself; you are (or seem to be) reading, but actually you are praying. The patristic texts in particular lend themselves to this type of reading because they are filled with quotes from scripture or with scriptural allusions. But some modern readings can elicit the same.

Thus, in reading such texts, you are feeding the inner spirit and you are praying. In addition, the texts prompt many beautiful thoughts, ideas, and prayers. One cannot just read the text and put it aside; the text stays with you and leads you to greater depths of thought and prayer. This is *lectio divina*—literally, divine or sacred reading.

A medieval writer in the book *Meditations of Saint Augustine* depicts well this notion of *lectio divina:*

> I love to raise the eyes of my heart to you, elevate my mind to you, and shape the affections of my soul to harmonize with you. I love to speak and hear and write and converse about you, daily to read of your glorious blessedness, and frequently to mull over in my heart what I have read of you. In this way I am able to turn from the passions and dangers and labors of this mortal and transitory life to the sweet coolness of your life-giving breezes and, when I so turn, to rest my weary head, even if only for a moment, on your bosom. It is for this

---

2. J. E. Rotelle, ed., *Tradition Day by Day* (Villanova: Augustinian Press, 1994).

purpose that I enter the pleasing fields of the sacred scriptures, there to find and pluck the fresh growth of its sentences, to eat by reading and digest by frequent meditation, and finally to gather them all into the deep storehouse of my memory.

How To Use This Book

One could pick up this book and read it from cover to cover, but I doubt if that person would derive much from that reading. The best way to use this book is twofold: First, you could read it in conjunction with the Sunday gospel in the proper cycle, that is, Year A, B, or C. Or, secondly, one who preaches could use it as background for a homily or sermon; others could use it in preparation for the Sunday celebration. The book could be used as a source of meditation either for each Sunday, or in preparation for the Sunday, or for some days during the year.

Inclusive Language

The readings range from the seventeenth to the twentieth centuries. Some are translations; others were written in English— English of different eras, a Cardinal Newman English to a Gerald Vann style.

Wherever possible, inclusive language has been the goal without detriment, however, to the meaning. At times it was easy, changing man to human being, men to men and women; at other times it was not so easy, and at times changes could not be made because the male or female (as in the case of Julian of Norwich) imagery was embedded in the text.

It is my hope that this florilegium of texts will help you to deepen your living of the gospel life and to provide you with moments of prayerful reading and revelation.

John E. Rotelle, O.S.A.

Readings

First Sunday of Advent

Gospel: Mark 13:33-37

Jesus said to his disciples: "Be constantly on the watch! Stay awake! You do not know when the appointed time will come."

Commentary: J.H. Newman

Before Christ came, the faithful remnant of Israel were consoled with the promise that "their eyes should see" him, who was to be their "salvation." "Unto you that fear my name shall the Sun of righteousness arise with healing in his wings." Yet it is observable that the prophecy, though cheering and encouraging, had with it something of an awful character too.

This reflection leads us to a parallel thought concerning the state and prospects of all Christians in every age. We who are looking out for Christ's coming, we are bid to look out, we are bid to pray for it; and yet it is to be a time of judgment. It is to be the deliverance of all saints from sin and sorrow for ever; yet they, every one of them, must undergo an awful trial. How then can any look forward to it with joy, not knowing (for no one knows) the certainty of his own salvation? And the difficulty is increased when we come to pray for it, to pray for its coming soon: how can we pray that Christ would come, that the day of judgment would hasten, that his kingdom would come, that his kingdom may be at once, may come on us this day or tomorrow, when by so coming he would be shortening the time of our present life, and cut off those precious years given us for conversion, amendment, repentance, and sanctification? Is there not an inconsistency in professing to wish our judge already come, when we do not feel ourselves ready for him? In what sense can we really and heartily pray that he would cut short the time, when our conscience tells us that, even were our life longest, we should have much to do in a few years?

When we pray for the coming of Christ, we do but pray in the Church's words, that he would "*accomplish the number* of his elect and would hasten his kingdom." That is, we do not pray that he would simply cut short the world, but, so to express myself, that he would make time go quicker, and the wheels of his chariot speed on. Before he comes, a certain space must be gone over; all the saints must be gathered in, and each saint must be matured. Not a grain must fall to the ground; not an ear of corn must lose its due rain and sunshine. All we pray is that he would please to crowd all this into a short space of time; that he would "finish the work and cut it short in *righteousness*," and "make a short work upon the earth"; that he would accomplish — not curtail, but fulfill — the circle of his saints, and hasten the age to come without disordering this. Indeed it cannot be otherwise. All God's works are in place and season; they are all complete. As in nature, the structure of its minutest portions is wrought out to perfection, and an insect is as wonderful as Leviathan; so, when in his providence he seems to hurry, he still keeps time, and moves upon the deep harmonies of truth and love. When then we pray that he would come, we pray also that we may be ready; that all things may converge and meet in him; that he may draw us while he draws near us, and makes us the holier the closer he comes. We pray that we may not fear that which at present we justly fear; *that when he shall appear, we may have confidence, and not be ashamed before him at his coming.*

(*Parochial and Plain Sermons* V, 46-51)

John Henry Newman (1801-1890) was born in London and brought up in the Church of England. He went up to Trinity College, Oxford, in 1817, became a Fellow of Oriel five years later, was ordained a deacon in 1824 and appointed vicar of Saint Mary's, Oxford, in 1832. The impact of his sermons was tremendous. He was the leading spirit in the Tractarian Movement (1833-1841) and the condemnation of "Tract 90" led to his resignation from Saint Mary's in 1843. Two years later he was received into the Catholic Church. He was ordained in Rome and founded a house of Oratorians in Birmingham. Newman's *Essay on the Development of Christian Doctrine* throws light on his withdrawal of previous objections to Roman Catholicism; his *Apologia* reveals the deepest motives underlying his outward attitudes, and *The Grammar of Assent* clarifies the subjective content of commitment to faith. In 1879 he was made a cardinal and he died at Edgbaston in 1890.

Second Sunday of Advent

Gospel: Mark 1:1-8

Here begins the gospel of Jesus Christ, the Son of God. In Isaiah the prophet it is written: "I sent my messenger before you to prepare your way."

Commentary: E. Schillebeeckx

*I*n today's story from the gospel of Mark, John the Baptist is this *angelos*, messenger and forerunner. He introduces the chief character in the story: Jesus of Nazareth. Moreover he explains to the public, his readers, who this Jesus really is. The performers — the disciples and the other Jews — are still ignorant of this at this stage in the story. The tension in the story is in fact produced by the fact that they are ignorant, whereas the audience is aware of what is going on. So the messenger seeks to prepare the audience for the entry of the main character, whose secret he reveals to them beforehand. Afterwards this messenger disappears from the stage.

To understand this short passage properly, and also to grasp what it means for us, above all now in the season of Advent, we need to see that it is in fact made up of a web of all kinds of reminiscences of Old Testament texts: Exodus, Malachi, and Isaiah. These texts prompted all kinds of messianic expectations in the time of Jesus. For the Jews it was a time of crisis. But they looked for a new Moses and a new liberation. This expectation was bound up with the coming appearance of a Moses-like messenger, bringing good news, who would first proclaim aloud the approaching event of liberation.

In Christianity, Mark's message tells us today, we are indeed concerned with liberation. But as in the first deliverance from Egypt under Moses, in the second exodus from Babylon, and finally, in the definitive deliverance brought about by Jesus, for us the "work of liberation" means going through the wilderness: that is the way in which we can be certain that God goes with us and that we are not risking some solitary adventure with an ideological "God with us."

16

We may leave open the question whether consistent Christian action may ever get us into prison. At all events, our work of liberation is not a smooth, obvious triumphal course in Babylonian style. Given the geography of our world, the *condition humaine* of our human existence, we shall in fact have constantly to keep going through the wilderness if we are to bring about some liberation for others and to taste something of the savor of liberation for ourselves.

Finally, what is striking about both the book of Isaiah and Mark is that neither of these prophet-forerunners calls himself a liberation-through-another. They both feel themselves to us useless servants, however necessary they may be, because it will have struck you that in this prologue to Mark our attention is drawn to the historical appearance of Jesus in our world by a third person: an eccentrically dressed young man with the "hair shirt" characteristic of a prophet and the "leather girdle" typical of Elijah: in other words a fool. By contrast, Jesus, the all-important figure, makes an unobtrusive appearance, in the usual clothes of the ordinary person of his time. You could very well pass him by, had there not been this unusual man to point a finger at him. Jesus' coming to and among us is so unobtrusive that he could remain unknown in our history were we not constantly, time and again, endlessly, to proclaim him and point a finger to him (perhaps being rejected by the world, like the Baptist, as crazy). That is the reason why our Dominican order exists and it is also the task for our ministry and for all Christians in their lives: to do what the prophet Isaiah and what John the Baptist did. For God is always a God who is to come — that is his name and nature — always in a different and a new way according to the different circumstances in which we live. He therefore always needs humble and yet daring forerunners.

(The Way to Freedom, 3-7)

Edward Schillebeeckx (1914-) was born in Antwerp, the Netherlands, and entered the Domincan Order and was ordained in 1941. He studied at the Dominican Faculty of Theology of the Saulchoir, École des Hauts Études, and the Sorbonne in Paris, France, earning a doctorate of theology in 1951 and a master of theology in 1959. He was professor of systematic theology at the University of Nijmegen from 1958 until his retirement. He has published many books and has shaped the future of theology.

Third Sunday of Advent

Gospel: John 1:6-8.19-28

There was a man named John sent by God, who came as a witness to testify to the light, so that through him all might believe.

Commentary: J. Daniélou

As John the Baptist was the Lord's precursor even before his birth, so also he was the forerunner of Christ's public life. After the desert period came the crowning moment of a life spent preparing the way for Christ. *There was a man sent from God whose name was John. This man came as a witness, to give testimony to the light, so that all might come to believe through him. He himself was not the light; his task was to bear witness to the light.*

This text shows that the essential mission of John the Baptist was to bear witness to the light, to point to Jesus. His was a pre-eminent role in the preparation for the coming of Christ and of Christ's own work. John it was who paved the way for our Lord's public life and teaching by predisposing the souls of his hearers to receive it. One might say he was an educator of souls; his task was as it were to rough-hew them, to do the preliminary chiseling that would make them more receptive to Christ's message. Our Lord's teaching would have been too strong for souls not previously prepared for it. They needed some schooling in advance. Their interests had to be re-directed; it was necessary to wean them from worldly habits and to arouse a spiritual dissatisfaction in their hearts.

That was John the Baptist's assignment. Sent to people utterly heedless of the things of God, it was his task to awaken in them sufficient concern to disturb their settled ways and to stir up their initial goodwill, so that they might be capable of understanding Christ.

John the Baptist thus joins the long succession of those who have taken part in the work of preparing for the Lord's coming, those who, like John, were withdrawn by God from the things of this world and mysteriously admitted to the divine plans, in order that they might blaze the way for God among the people. John in his turn will move among his contemporaries to mark out the Lord's way, smoothing paths and leveling hills. But for such a mission he must from the outset be possessed by the Lord in the depths of his being, since it is a hard furrow he will have to plow. The people of the Baptist's generation were absorbed in the same pursuits as the people of our own day. Saint Luke describes them in a memorable passage, the soldiers engaged in violence and false charges, and the tax collectors in demanding more than their due.

Such is human nature. It was so in the time of John, and it is the same today. Preoccupied with worldly affairs, people are completely heedless of God. As one goes here and there in the world it is very painful to experience the utter indifference of the rank and file. To shake the world out of this divine vision, who can rouse the masses from their inertia. They have to be authentic witnesses. A witness is someone who has first been granted an inner vision; God has introduced him to the divine viewpoint so that he can pass on what he has seen to others.

So it was with John the Baptist. God first admitted him to his own counsel, revealing to him the mystery of the divine plan, drawing him into the desert to share with him his own joy. Then came the essential part of his vocation: he was a witness to Christ, that is to say he was the one who pointed out Christ to the people.

(*Le mystère de l'Avent*, 82-84)

Jean Daniélou (1905-1974), born into a privileged family, his father being a politican and his mother an educationalist, did brilliantly at his studies, and in 1929 entered the Society of Jesus. He came under the influence of de Lubac and got to know Teilhard de Chardin. In 1940 he was chaplain to students in Paris and committed to the cause of resistance. Widely ecumenical in his views, he was a peritus at Vatican II under Pope John XXIII, and was made a cardinal by Pope Paul VI. As an author he was at home in many fields of erudition, including scripture, patristics, theology, and spirituality.

Fourth Sunday of Advent

Gospel: Luke 1:26-38

The angel Gabriel was sent from God to a town of Galilee named Nazareth, to a virgin betrothed to a man named Joseph, of the house of David. The virgin's name was Mary.

Commentary: G. Vann

*I*n the Church's devotion to Mary great emphasis is laid on the fact that in her motherhood she yet remained a maiden as well; and we shall miss all the richness of the mystery if we think of this insistence as being purely or even primarily concerned with physical conditions. Motherhood produces fundamental psychological changes in a woman: it means the loss of some qualities and the acquisition of others, a different mentality, a different outlook. The mother has known the deep experience of love and joy, of pain and danger and sorrow: we think of her as the symbol of wisdom because she has known in her own body the mysteries of good and evil. The girl on the other hand is the symbol of opposite qualities: of a freshness and spontaneity and purity of heart which come precisely from inexperience, knowing only that reality can be ugly, not yet made wise through lessons of sorrow: her courage, her strength, her wisdom, her joy, are from other sources. In Mary alone, the Maiden-Mother, these opposite sets of qualities co-exist; it is this that gives her personality a richness which is unique; and it is because of this richness that she can teach us so much.

Mary's life then is a song at once of innocence and of experience; and as this double richness means a double fear so it means also a double love; and the love in its turn produces a double wisdom, a double trust, and therefore a double courage. Mary pondered all these things in her heart: it is her song of experience, and the source of her mother-wisdom. She knew how he that is mighty had done great things in her; she knew the overshadowing power of the most high; she knew the gradually unfolding self-revelation of her Son; and knowing these things she could sense the resurrection through the cross, the joy through the pain, the triumph through failure; and so she could find the courage to meet the sword. *Behold the handmaid of the Lord*: there, on the other hand, is her song of innocence: whatever may come it will be well because it is his will, because he is Love: hers are eyes too that can look out untroubled on a future which is veiled, simply because she has implicit trust in the God she loves, even before the trust has been justified by experience; and as the mother can say, I can do all things in him who has strengthened me, so the girl can say, I can do all things in him who will strengthen me.

(*The Son's Course*, 60-62)

Gerald Vann (1906-1963) was educated by Dominicans and in 1923 entered the Order. He was ordained six years later. His studies took him first to Rome and then to Oxford. He then went to Laxton as a member of a teaching staff and afterward became headmaster and superior of the house. He was a prolific author with a special gift for conveying profound truths in a very readable way to a wide public. He was interested in the moral problem of war, and as early as 1936 founded a Union of Prayer for Peace.

Christmas

Gospel: Luke 2:1-14

In those days Caesar Augustus published a decree ordering a census of the whole world.

Commentary: G.K. Chesterton

The human story began in a cave; the cave which popular science associates with the cave-man and in which practical discovery has really found archaic drawings of animals. The second half of human history, which was like a new creation of the world, also begins in a cave. There is even a shadow of such a fancy in the fact that animals were again present; for it was a cave used as a stable by the mountaineers of the uplands about Bethlehem; who still drive their cattle into such holes and caverns at night. It was here that a homeless couple had crept underground with the cattle when the doors of the crowded caravanserai had been shut in their faces; and it was here beneath the very feet of the passers-by, in a cellar under the very floor of the world, that Jesus Christ was born. But in that second creation there was indeed something symbolical in the roots of the primeval rock or the horns of the prehistoric hero. God also was a Cave-Man, and had also traced strange shapes of creatures, curiously colored, upon the wall of the world; but the pictures that he made had come to life. A mass of legend and literature had repeated and rung the changes on that single paradox; that the hands that had made the sun and stars were too small to reach the huge heads of the cattle.

Christ was not only born on the level of the world, but even lower than the world. The first act of the divine drama was enacted, not only on no stage set above the sightseer, but on a drab and curtained stage sunken out of sight; and that is an idea very difficult to express in most modes of artistic expression. It is the idea of simultaneous happenings on different levels of life. Perhaps it could have been best conveyed by the characteristic expedient of some of the medieval guilds, when they wheeled about the streets a theatre with three stages one above the other, with heaven above the earth and hell under the earth. But in the riddle of Bethlehem it was heaven that was under the earth.

All this indescribable thing that we call the Christmas atmosphere only hangs in the air as something like a lingering fragrance or fading vapor from the exultant explosion of that one hour in the Judean hills nearly two thousand years ago. But the savior is still unmistakable, and it is something too subtle to be covered by our use of the word peace. By the very nature of the story the rejoicings in the cavern were rejoicings in a fortress or an outlaw's den; properly understood it is not unduly flippant to say that they were rejoicings in a dug-out. It is not only true that such a subterranean chamber was a hiding-place from enemies; and that the enemies were already scouring the stony plain that lay above it like a sky. It is not only that the very horse-hoofs of Herod might in that sense have passed like thunder over the sunken head of Christ. It is also that there is in that image a true idea of an outpost, of a piercing through the rock and an entrance into an enemy territory. There is in this buried divinity an idea of *undermining* the world; of shaking the towers and palaces from below; even as Herod the great king felt that earthquake under him and swayed with his swaying palace.

(*The Writings*, 64-65)

Gilbert Keith Chesterton (1874-1936) was born in Campden Hill, London, England. He was a famous English novelist, poet, critic, essayist, journalist, biographer, history, and short story writer. Attracted to Catholicism at an early age he was received into the Catholic Church in 1922. He is most known for his Father Brown short stories, five volumes published between 1911 and 1935. He died in England in 1936.

Holy Family

Gospel: Luke 2:22-40

When the day came to purify them according to the law of Moses, Mary and Joseph brought Jesus up to Jerusalem so that he could be presented to the Lord.

Commentary: C. Carretto

Of all the men and women who lived by faith, two reached towering heights. They lived at the watershed between the Old and New Testaments and were called by God to such a unique and magnificent vocation that heaven was made to wait in suspense for their reply: Mary and Joseph.

Mary became the mother of the Word; she gave flesh and blood to the Son of God; and Joseph must veil the mystery, placing himself at her side so that everyone might believe that Jesus was his son. For these two creatures the night of faith was not only dark, but also painful.

One day Joseph, engaged to Mary, realizes that she is to give birth to a child which he knows is not his. Think of the task of convincing one's betrothed that the mystery of that birth is due to nothing less than the power of God. No reasoning could give Joseph peace and serenity. Only faith. And it is precisely this faith which sustained him, placing him next to the mother of God, to accompany her in her destiny and take a full part in her mission. It won't be easy to follow the example of such a man destined to suffer, the spouse of a woman who is to be called the Mother of Sorrows.

The baby is born. A few angels came, it is true, to chase away a little of that darkness, but at once the sky closed on a yet greater darkness. The children of the entire village are slain on account of their baby, and Joseph and Mary, fleeing, hear the cry and lament of the women of Bethlehem.

Why? Why is the All-Powerful silent? Why doesn't he kill Herod? But this is the point: it is necessary to live by faith. Flee into Egypt, become exiles and refugees, let cruelty and injustice triumph. And so it will be until the end of time.

God didn't soften the path of those whom he put beside his Son. He asked of them a faith so pure and uncompromising that only two souls could live up to this demand. What an adventure, to live for thirty years in a house where God lived in the flesh of an earthly man; to eat with him, listen to him speak, see him sleep, see the sweat on his brow, and on his hands the callouses of weariness and work.

And all this quite simply, as something normal and everyday; so normal that absolutely nobody will unveil the mystery or realize that the carpenter's son is the Son of God, the Word made flesh, the new Adam, heaven and earth.

My God, what great faith!

Mary and Joseph, you it is who are masters of faith, perfect examples to inspire us, correct our course, and support our weakness.

Just as you were beside Jesus, you are still beside us to accompany us to eternal life, to teach us to be small and poor in our work, humble and hidden in life, courageous in trial, faithful in prayer, and ardent in love.

And when the hour of our death comes and dawn rises over our friendly night, our eyes, as they scan the sky, may pick out the same star that was in your sky when Jesus came upon earth.

(*Letters from the Desert*, 144-146)

Carlo Carretto (1910-1988), born in Alessandria, Italy, received his degree in philosophy from the University of Turin in 1932. During the Fascist era he was confined to Sardinia, and in the turbulent years following the war he served as national president of Catholic Youth in Italy from 1946-1952. At the age of forty-four he left Italy for North Africa, where he joined the Little Brothers without knowing anything of their rules, and embraced the way of life of Charles de Foucauld, of whom he had not previously heard. Born of Carretto's solitude and contemplation, *Letters from the Desert* was an instant success in Italy, where it has gone through twenty-four editions.

Mary, Mother of God

Gospel: Luke 2:16-21

The shepherds went in haste to Bethlehem and found Mary and Joseph, and the baby lying in the manger.

Commentary: L.J. Suenens

An unparalleled human adventure, this is our modern world. One need only consider space exploration with all its possibilities and connotations. And these external discoveries do not stand alone. Science probes more and more deeply into the human organism itself. Perhaps tomorrow it will remold and refashion human beings according to its own blueprint. All this is at once tremendous and frightening.

Yet though science opens up infinite horizons, it cannot answer the most elementary and vital questions that people still ask themselves: What is the ultimate meaning of this human adventure and of our life here below? What awaits us after death, even supposing death could be artificially postponed at will? This is the real human anxiety, this the question each person is asking.

There must be an answer to these questions, at all costs there must. To multiply ways and techniques for keeping ourselves alive will not suffice. We need more fundamental motives for going on living.

It is here that Mary appears, offering her Son to humanity as the one who alone possesses the words of eternal life. We find Mary at the very heart of the mystery of the incarnation. She is the mother of the one who will be for all future ages the way, the truth, and the life. The threshold of the one who, above all, can introduce us to Jesus. The story of the Wise Kings is no mere page of past history; it is a symbol of the ongoing quest of the human race. The Magi set out through desert and darkness, eyes fixed upon the light which would eventually lead them to Bethlehem. The gospel describes them entering the house and finding the child with Mary his mother. They fell down and adored him. It was through meeting the mother of our Savior that they discovered Christ.

One cannot see the child apart from his mother, nor the mother apart from the child; for the mystery of the incarnation only yields its full meaning through the faithful cooperation and humble willingness of her whom tradition calls *Theotokos*.

Today's world needs to rediscover the face of its Savior and of his mother. The world is glutted with philosophies and ideologies which, no matter what they have to offer, do not answer its most vital need, its most fundamental questions. To our contemporary world Mary offers the living and vibrant reality, the incarnate Savior of the world. She offers overwhelming proof that Christ is not, as we sometimes unconsciously imagine, a being part God and part man, but that he is wholly divine and totally human.

Mary is the safeguard of the realism of the incarnation.

"Marie et le monde d'aujourd'hui"

("Marie et le monde d'aujourd'hui," *Documentation Catholique* [1971] 878-879.)

Leon Joseph Suenens (1904-1996) was born in Brussels, Belgium, and after having entered the seminary he studied at the Gregorian University in Rome and earned a doctorate in theology in 1927. After ordination as a priest in 1927 he taught at the seminary from 1930-1940. From 1940-1945 he taught philosophy at the seminary in Malines, Belgium, and was auxiliary bishop (1945-1961) and the archbishop of Malines from 1961. He was very prominent at the Second Vatican Council and in the post-conciliar era of Vatican II.

Second Sunday after Christmas

Gospel: John 1:1-18

In the beginning was the Word; the Word was in God's presence, and the Word was God.

Commentary: R. Voillaume

Jesus appears in the world without giving any warning of his coming and without making known to any neighbor who he is. Had he come into the world in his house at Nazareth, all his relatives would have made an event of his birth with the neighbors and the other inhabitants of the town. He would have been heralded and celebrated. He would thus have allowed himself to behave well enough like a true little Nazarene, but he would have been confiscated, as it were, by his earthly family and his earthly country. Quite to the contrary, he elects to be born away from home, on a journey, amid an anonymous crowd; in this way, he would really belong to everybody, and could come quietly and discreetly, with no tumult and excitement. God, if he had so wished, could naturally have made all sorts of efforts to spread the news abroad. And if any proof were needed of this, one could point to his having mobilized the angels but contented himself with bringing a few poor shepherds to the manger. It is also clear from this that he could easily have brought the whole of Jerusalem and all the just among the Israelites with pure and upright hearts, worshipers of God and living in expectancy of the Messiah. And there were in fact many of them, all true friends of his, in the country of Judea and Galilee!

But it is obvious that God did not wish to impose his Son: people must come to him by seeking and discovering him. Even the shepherds and the Wise Men, though warned personally, had to search for him with the help of a sign which, rather than leading them easily and directly to the manger, was little more than a suggestion to send them on their way. The shepherds must have gone to many houses and stables before they found the right babe wrapped in swaddling clothes.

As for the Magi, they had to show some initiative in order to discover, by the normal means at their disposal, the birthplace of the young king of Israel. Jesus was infinitely discreet; he simply waited, and such a way of appearing could have made us somewhat impatient, had it not been proved for centuries back that men have found in this very discretion a true sign of God. That sign of weakness, which draws men in spite of themselves, makes them surrender and acknowledge themselves outdone, without Jesus ever having forced himself upon them in any way other than a certain presence — a presence that waits, and invites, and demonstrates God's heaven in a humble manner which gives hope and humility, peace and love — just how, one does not really know! God is a master who knows how to go about speaking to us with the use of the things of earth — these various beings, both animate and inanimate — and the events of humanity's history.

("The Time of the Nativity" *Jesus Christ* [1964] 28-29)

Réné Voillaume (1905-) founded the first fraternity of the Little Brothers of Jesus in October 1933 in El Abiodh in the Sahara Desert. His spirituality follows that of Father de Foucauld and is eminently based on the gospel. Voillaume has the gift of discovering the face of the suffering Christ in the poor.

Epiphany

Gospel: Matthew 2:1-12

After Jesus' birth in Bethlehem of Judea during the reign of King Herod, astrologers from the east arrived one day in Jerusalem inquiring, "Where is the newborn king of the Jews?"

Commentary: A. Löhr

*T*he feast of Epiphany to some extent foreshadows our Lord's passion and the glory of Easter, and so completes the message of Christmas. At Epiphany we celebrate three events in the life of Jesus which reveal him to the world as incarnate Lord, God, and King: the adoration of the newborn child by Wise Men, the baptism of Jesus in the Jordan, and the marriage at Cana. The star, that ancient symbol of kings (and of gods too, because the ancients believed that kings were the descendants of gods), reveals the divine kingship of the penniless child in Bethlehem to the wise men of the east. At Jesus' baptism in the Jordan the Father testifies that the man Jesus is his divine Son, and the power of God descends on him visibly in the form of a dove. The miracle of the wine at Cana reveals the divine authority of Jesus in his absolute command over the created world.

Behold, our Lord and King has come, and in his hand are power and authority! The ruler is here, and the world throngs toward him. That is the picture which the reading from Isaiah paints for us. But it is only a picture, not a recording of historical fact. The obscurity of Jesus' first coming prevented the people from greeting him as Lord. The prophet's vision unrolls before us a picture of that mysterious power which the transfigured Christ has exercised over human minds ever since his resurrection. As the "being to whom alone love is due" he is unique, and even the hatred of his enemies has now become a tribute.

There is also a vivid picture here of Christ's second coming at the end of the world, when he will reveal himself as the mysterious power at work in the universe, the sole being in whose hands lie the threads of all human destiny and time. *Our Lord and King!* In that final epiphany of his divine glory he will conquer the whole world. It is this event which is already mysteriously present to us in our celebration today. A straight line runs from the judgment of the first Sunday of Advent to the glory of the Epiphany. *Arise, shine out, Jerusalem, for the glory of the Lord has shed its light upon you!* At the dawn Mass of Christmas we glimpsed the return of our lost paradise which today appears in its full regal splendor. Standing beside Christ the King we see his bride, the Church, in increasing glory. Flooded by his light, she recognizes him and hastens toward him. A bride indeed, she is at the same time the virgin mother of many children. *Her sons will come from far away and her daughters will be carried in men's arms.* Of her the peoples of the world are born to new life. Her womb is the baptismal water, consecrated and made fruitful by the Spirit of the Lord. That is why, next to Easter, the Epiphany is the second of the Church's great baptismal feasts. *See, here I am with the children the Lord has given me!*

"No longer is it gold, incense, and myrrh that we offer you; we offer and receive instead what those gifts signify: Jesus Christ, your Son, our Lord."

(Das Herrenjahr I, 122-127)

Ämiliana Löhr (1896-1972) studied philosophy, literature, and history of art at Cologne. During her studies she felt a call to the monastic life, and in 1927 entered the Abbey of the Holy Cross, a new foundation of Benedictine nuns at Herstelle on the Weser, where she took vows in 1931. She was allowed to continue writing as far as the life in the Benedictine community permitted it. Unusually gifted, she published many essays, reports, and poems dealing with literary, contemporary, hagiographical, and liturgical themes. The most important theme of her writings, however, is the liturgy grounded in the theology of Odo Casel, O.S.B., which was practiced in her abbey. The intention of her first work, *The Mass through the Year (Das Herrenjahr)*, was to make people personally and truly participate in Jesus' work of salvation. The book met with a lively response, had six editions, and was translated into English. Her books on the hymns and Holy Week are evidence of a liturgy practiced in everyday life; even after the reform of the breviary they are still a rich source of information for liturgists.

31

Baptism of the Lord

Gospel: Mark 1:7-11   The theme of John's preaching was: "One more powerful than I is to come after me."

Commentary: F. Durrwell

The theophany of the Jordan marks the beginning of Christ's public life. God guarantees Jesus of Nazareth: the voice from heaven shows that he is the Son; the presence of the Holy Spirit shows that he is the Messiah, the Anointed One of Yahweh, upon whom the power of God rests. Like the heroes of old, Christ enters upon his career by the impetus of the Holy Spirit. This is the meaning of the theophany; but the baptism of our Lord, taken as a whole, has a larger and more complex significance.

John was the herald going ahead to open the road, the friend leading the way. The justice he must fulfill was preparing the road and ushering in his great friend. The justice Christ must fulfill was to be the Savior of the sinful people. The meeting between them brought John to the culminating point of his mission as he ushered Christ into his work of redemption. The baptism was the prelude to the redemption, and there lies its mystery.

It was a prelude in symbol as well as in reality, for the whole act of redemption was reflected in it and begun in it. Our Lord must place himself among sinners and submit to "baptism unto penance." He was later to submit to another baptism: *I have a baptism wherewith I am to be baptized. Can you be baptized with the baptism wherewith I am to be baptized?* His immersion in the water of penance was an anticipation and a figure of the blood and suffering of that other baptism. Corresponding to that momentary humiliation there was a glorification: *And Jesus, being baptized, came up out of the water; and behold a voice from heaven saying, This is my beloved Son in whom I am well pleased.* Jesus came up out of the Jordan as later he was to rise from the dead, in the glory of the Spirit, in the manifestation of the divine sonship; the new creation which was to be fulfilled in the resurrection was already promised.

The baptism of water to which Christ had to submit himself was, therefore, related to his essential work of death and resurrection; it is, as it were, a preliminary sketch of the work of redemption. From then onward John the Baptist, who had not known him before except as a judge to be feared, called him the *Lamb of God who takes away the sin of the world*. It is also significant that this anticipation of the drama of the redemption took place in a ritual of water: Christ was rehearsing for his death and resurrection by entering the waters of baptism and emerging from them.

(*The Resurrection*, 314-315)

Francis X. Durrwell (1912-), a Redemptorist born in Alsace, is characterized by the total honesty with which he views the sacred text. Having chosen to pursue a biblical and historical theology, he does not accommodate the word of God to the exposition of his point of view, but submits his researches to the enlightenment to be attained by scriptural witnesses. He also was superior of his province in Strasbourg and is best known for his work *The Resurrection*.

First Sunday of Lent

Gospel: Mark 1:12-15

The Spirit sent Jesus out toward the desert. He stayed in the wasteland forty days, put to the test there by Satan.

Commentary: A. de Orozco

Beloved, I beg you, let us accompany our king, Christ Jesus, and seek out the wilderness of repentance as quickly as we can. Let us be ashamed from now on to spare time for pleasures and gluttony, while our Savior is engaged in prayer and lengthy fasting. With Uriah, that upright soldier, let us say: *The ark of God dwells in tents, and my lord Joab is in camp fighting against the enemy*, and shall we apply ourselves to pleasures? We must blush when we see how Jesus Christ, the ark of God, *in which are hidden all the treasures of the wisdom and knowledge of God*, is joining battle with the devil in the wilderness, while we take our leisure and seek fleshly delights. Let us bravely resist the tempter and tell him: *Not on bread alone does man live but on every word that comes from the mouth of God*. Let us rely always on him who gives food to all flesh and does not forget the crows when they call on him, and we shall overcome that vilest of vices, gluttony. Let us perform our actions for the glory of God and do everything in praise of the Creator, and let us not tempt God Most Good, for it is written: *You shall not tempt the Lord your God*, and again: *Whoever loves danger will perish in it*. If we keep this in mind, we shall be able to escape vainglory.

Finally, if the wicked king of Babylon erects a golden statue on a high mountain and offers many possessions, power, and riches, and if we are not careful, we shall adore a monster, namely, the statue of the devil, as many do. Let us rather imitate the courage of the three young men and enter the fiery furnace by embracing poverty of spirit, for it is written: *The Lord your God shall you adore, and him only shall you serve*. The angel of the Lord will certainly come and turn the middle of the fiery furnace into a place where the moist wind blows, and the fire shall not be able to harm us.

Instead, we shall claim the victory over the enemy and shall with one voice and one heart sing unwearying praises and countless thanksgivings to Christ our King, for he has rescued us from so many dangers and won a glorious victory over an aggressive foe. Finally, by the gift of his grace he has cast down the supporter of the proud, so that he might promote us, his athletes, and raise us up to heavenly glory. To him be endless praise and rule with the Father and the Holy Spirit. Amen.

(First Sunday of Lent, *Sermon 1, Opera Omnia* I, 239)

Alonso de Orozco, O.S.A. (1500-1591) studied at the University of Salamanca before entering the Augustinian novitiate there. His main apostolates in the Order were preaching and writing, and although he was chosen as royal preacher at the Spanish court, he preferred to speak to poor and simple people. His religious life was marked by a spirit of fraternity, gospel simplicity, and moderation in speech. As an ascetic and great mystic, he suffered crisis and spiritual aridity from 1522 to 1551. He was beatified by Pope Leo XIII in 1882.

Second Sunday of Lent

Gospel: Mark 9:2-10

Jesus took Peter, James, and John off by themselves with him and led them up a high mountain. He was transfigured before their eyes.

Commentary: C. Marmion

What we see in the transfiguration is a revelation of our own future greatness. We shall participate in Christ's glory. How can this be? Because he gives to us, his members, the right to share in the inheritance he possesses as the very Son of God. Listen to the thought of Saint Leo: "By this mystery of the transfiguration, God's wonderful providence has laid the foundations of the Church's hope, teaching the whole body of Christ the nature of the transformation it is to undergo, and schooling his members to look forward to a share in the glory which has already shone out in their head."

Even here below, we are God's children by grace; but what we are going to become as a result of this adoption has not yet appeared. It will happen when "his lightnings have lit up the whole world, shaking the earth to its foundations," and the justified, according to our Lord's own words, will arise to glory. *They will shine like the sun in the kingdom of their Father.* Their bodies will be resplendent like that of Christ on Tabor; they will be transfigured by the very same clarity that illumines the incarnate Word. Saint Paul tells us clearly: *He will refashion this lowly body of ours, conforming it to the likeness of his own glorified body.*

We should not, of course, assume that on the holy mountain the sacred humanity was endowed with all the splendor now beaming from it in heaven. The disciples saw only a single ray of that glory, yet it was enough to lift them out of themselves. This marvelous radiance came from the divinity. It was an overflowing of the Godhead on the sacred humanity. Eternal life was always hidden in Christ, but at this hour something of that light flamed out from its glowing center and set his very body on fire. It was no borrowed light, coming from without, but rather a manifestation of that ineffable majesty always contained and concealed within our Lord. For love of us, Jesus during his earthly existence usually hid the divine life that was in him under the guise of mortal flesh and blood. He would not let it overflow in a continual brilliance that could have impaired our frail vision. But at the transfiguration the Word set his glory free to irradiate the humanity he had assumed.

This should convince us that holiness consists in our likeness to Christ Jesus, the flowing through us of the divine life, not a perfection we achieve of ourselves. Our baptism was the dawning in us of this holiness, through the grace of Christ. *God predestined us to be conformed to the image of his Son.* Little by little this likeness grows, if we are faithful to the action of the Holy Spirit, deepening and developing even to the fullness of eternal life. Then the angels and all the elect will be able to see the transformation that has taken place; for us, an inexhaustible spring of joy, and the supreme ratification of our divine adoption made perfect.

(*Le Christ dans ses mystères*, 332-333)

Columba (Joseph) Marmion (1858-1923) was born in Dublin and entered the seminary of Clonliffe and completed his studies at Rome, where he was ordained in 1881. He taught philosophy for a time, but on a visit to Maredsous he felt called to the monastic life and took the habit under the name of Columba. He spent several years at Mont-Cesar (Louvain) as prior and professor of theology and was given the post as abbot of Maredsous in 1909, which he held till his death. Dom Marmion was very human and saintly, but demanding in the guidance of souls. The trilogy, *Christ the Life of the Soul, Christ in His Mysteries*, and *Christ the Ideal of the Monk*, published from notes of his conferences, has been very influential among those concerned with the spiritual life. His teaching has the merit of centering spirituality and all ascetical effort on the person of Christ working in us through baptismal grace.

Third Sunday of Lent

Gospel: John 2:13-25

As the Jewish Passover was near, Jesus went up to Jerusalem. In the temple precincts he came upon people engaged in selling oxen, sheep, and doves, and others seated changing gold.

Commentary: A. Guillerand

When Jesus defended his Father's honor, he defended it as one who was nothing and had nothing to lose. Hence his immediacy of action and the compelling strength of his character, so astonishing at first sight. The way he cast out the traders from the temple, the way he briefly cleared himself when they protested and demanded his credentials, show him as a master not over-anxious about explaining his conduct but asserting his right to command. Later on he would give them his justification and credentials; at present he chose to act. He would honor his Father, and avenge his honor; he had no other object in view, and nothing else was of consequence for him.

But how wrong I am in trying to fathom such ineffable sentiments, and still more in trying to express them! The Son of God, infinite Being in the presence of infinite Being, God entering the temple of God, the true Light illumining those walls and courts, the Presence filling them and filled himself with quickening light. Yet in that presence, that radiance of infinite glory, creatures of a day, wholly occupied with trifles, with neither thought nor glance for him, chatter, trade, cheat each other as if in a market. Our Lord's reaction is a force, both physical and moral, an irresistible surge of Being's own fullness. Face to face with him, all these people who live only on the surface are terrified, overthrown, literally unmade, cut to pieces, thrown out of themselves as their merchandise is thrown out of the temple or strewn on the ground. Dust before that mighty breath, making whatever he wills of it! The Son, glory of his Father, has come to remind them of his Father's honor: *Take all that out; you shall not make my Father's home a house of trade.* The disorder that insults the heavenly Father is in the people themselves, who have forgotten the command: *You shall not.*... Such disorder is evil and the divine Son must react against it. He banishes from the temple what is out of place there, and he banishes from souls the darkness that intercepts the light. What human beings have stolen from the Father he restores to him: his house, and his honor in that house.

The people were not condemned but enlightened; they were struck down in order that they might receive the light. Transitory, inferior affairs were sacrificed to the higher interests of God, and to the people's own true interests which were identical with those of God. Jesus did not hesitate nor draw back, either before this sacrifice or before the opposition he foresaw, either before the consequences for himself or for those he would enlighten. We feel from the first stroke that only one thing counted for him: the divine glory, the manifestation of a Supreme Being who must be treated as such. Jesus saw nothing else; he was completely absorbed in this task, which was his own lifework.

(Au seuil de l'abîme de Dieu, 129-131)

Augustin Guillerand (1877-1945), born in Nivernais, France, was a parish priest until 1916 when he became attracted to the Carthusian way of life. As a Carthusian he became prior in 1935 of the monastery in Vedana, Italy. At the beginning of the Second World War he returned to France, and he and others began to live in the abandoned monastery Grande Chartreuse. It was here that he penned his meditations which were edited after his death.

Fourth Sunday of Lent

Gospel: John 3:14-21

Jesus said to Nicodemus: "Just as Moses lifted up the serpent in the desert, so must the Son of Man be lifted up, that all who believe may have eternal life in him."

Commentary: P. Bernard

The Savior comes to offer salvation not only to the Jews, but to the world: it is for this reason that he has been sent, indeed sacrificed. The judgment, with its throes and terrors, will subject to condemnation only those who truly reject the salvation offered to them. The believer, he who consents to be saved, will not be condemned: Jesus will say this more than once. On the other hand, the unbeliever, he who refuses to believe, is already judged. He is so by state of soul and differentiation of spirit: when the judgment will be made manifest, it will only uncover what each person bears in his heart. The discernment of spirits is realized according to whether or not they have believed in the name of him who is the Only-Begotten of God. God himself had no better envoy whom he could dispatch to us, nor any greater gift he could give us. There is no other name which can compare with this one. This is why the man who refuses to orientate his faith to this name has already condemned himself.

In speaking of the world as he does here, Jesus extends his thought far beyond the horizons of the Jews. He does not have merely the masters of Israel in view. He also casts his glance over the masters of the Gentiles. The maxims he enunciates are applicable to every region, as to all ages, of humanity. Jesus does not ask that, from the first stroke, everyone believe in him. He does not expect this, as we shall clearly see. The light of his revelation was not thus fashioned. It is a light of faith, a discreet light, which only achieves the day after passage through deep darknesses. He wishes only that individuals "come to this light," that they be willing to take the path toward him. The tragedy is that often they are unwilling, because of their works, which are worthless and which the light allows to be seen for what they are. This is grave for all, but particularly for those who are leaders and rulers, and even more so if they flatter themselves to be masters of thought, and principally of religious thought. Jesus knew what an immense danger overshadowed the world in this regard. What was happening in Israel as to the clouding of minds in matters of religious truth was taking place also among the nations. He lances then to the world this great and charitable warning in all its clarity. He who lives according to the truth, he concludes, literally "he who does the truth," the "poet" of the truth, betakes himself to the light.

What should we understand by this living in the truth, this "making of the truth"? What does Jesus mean? A very simple and beautiful thing. He does not mean that truth is in itself something which is fabricated and which anyone can bend to his way of thinking, mold to his manner, accommodate to his taste. He knows well that truth is a reality that is seen, that is sensed, which is taken as it is; the highest wisdom is to see it as God sees it. Jesus thinks of the man who applies himself to walking in righteousness and sincerity, of him who could be designated like Nathanael: this man sought to be true, to become true; in showing himself as he was, he did not dissimulate that which it would be necessary that he be; he made of his life a work of truth. Ah! this man, Jesus declares, is on his way to the light, he has nothing to hide; there is no darkness in him; his entire existence is transparent. This transparency reveals a presence and an inspiration of God, works accomplished in union with him.

(*The Mystery of Jesus*, volume 1, 66-67)

Pierre Bernard, O.P., a ranking French exegete and spiritual writer, has combined his talents in a justly heralded work about the Son of God: *The Mystery of Jesus*. Making use of the latest findings of modern scholarship together with a profound knowledge of human nature, the author has drawn a portrait of Jesus that has earned praise from critics and public alike; the work has been quickly translated into many other languages and has brought the mystery of Jesus home to countless modern readers.

Fifth Sunday of Lent

Gospel: John 12:20-33

Among those who had come up to worship at the feast of Passover were some Greeks. They approached Philip, who was from Bethsaida in Galilee, and put this request to him: "Sir, we should like to see Jesus."

Commentary: J. Ratzinger

The image of the passover, which is fulfilled in the New Testament of the death and resurrection; the image of the exodus, the leaving behind of one's possessions and the life to which one had become accustomed — an exodus which begins with Abraham and is the fundamental law of the whole of sacred history: all try to express this basic movement of auto-liberation from a purely selfish existence. Christ explained this in a more profound way in the law of the grain of wheat, which shows, at the same time, that this fundamental rule governs not only the whole of history, but also the whole of God's creation.

I tell you most solemnly, unless a wheat grain falls on the ground and dies, it remains only a single grain; but if it dies, it yields a rich harvest.

Christ, by his death and resurrection, fulfilled this law of the wheat grain. In the eucharist, the bread of God, he has truly become the hundredfold fruit on which we still live. But in this mystery of the eucharist, in which it is truly and fully he who lives for us, he asks us day after day to fulfill this law which is the definitive expression of the essence of true love. And so, the essential meaning of love can only be that we abandon our narrow and selfish aims and, coming out of ourselves, begin to live for others. In short, the fundamental movement of Christianity is none other than the simple basic movement of love, in which we participate in the creative love of God.

If we say, then, that the meaning of Christian service, the meaning of our faith, cannot be determined from the starting point of an individual belief but from the fact that we occupy a vital position in the whole and in relation to the whole; if it is true that we are not Christians for ourselves but because God wants and needs our service in the magnitude of history, then we will not fall into the error of thinking that the individual is only a small cog in the great machinery of the cosmos. Although it is true that God does not love merely the individual but everyone in mutual help and harmony, it is also true that he knows and loves each one of us as such. Jesus Christ, the Son of God and of man, in whom the decisive step in the universal history toward the union of creature with God was realized, was a concrete individual, born of a human mother. He lived his particular life, faced his own fate, and died his death. The scandal and the greatness of the Christian message is still that the destiny of the whole of history, our destiny, depends on the individual, on Jesus of Nazareth.

Seeing him as he is, both things become patently clear: that we should live for others and with their help, and that God, however, knows and loves each particular one of us with an unchanging love. I think that both things should profoundly impress us. On the one hand, we should apply the interpretation of Christianity as a way of life for the sake of others. But we should live, nonetheless, in the tremendous security and joy that God loves me, this person here; that he loves anyone who has a human face, however unrecognizable and profaned it might be. And when we say, "God loves me," we should not only feel the responsibility, the danger of making ourselves unworthy of that love, but we should accept that love and that grace in all its fullness and purity.

(Being Christian, 32-34)

Joseph Ratzinger (1927-) was ordained a priest for the diocese of Regensburg (1951), and was awarded his doctorate in theology from the University of Munich (1953) and served as professor of theology at the universities of Bonn (1959-1963), Münster (1963-1966), Tübingen (1966-1969), and Regensburg (1969-1977). During Vatican II, as a theological adviser to Cardinal Joseph Frings of Cologne, he was known for his progressive views. In March 1977, he was chosen by Paul VI to succeed Cardinal Julius Döpfner as the archbishop of Munich, and in June 1977 he was named a cardinal. In November 1981, he was appointed prefect of the Congregation for the Doctrine of the Faith by John Paul II, where he has led an effort to maintain doctrinal orthodoxy and clerical discipline in the post-Vatican II Church.

Passion Sunday
Palm Sunday

Gospel: Mark 14:1—15:47   The passion of our Lord Jesus Christ.

Commentary: A. de Orozco

I am glad to be able to show how deceitful the honors of this world are, for six days after the occasion of the palms the people of the same city turned around and accounted this same Lord among the wicked. What a difference between *Blessed is he who comes* and *Away with him! Away with him! Crucify him!* What a difference between *King of Israel* and *We have no king but Caesar; Give us Barabbas.* What a difference between the verdant branches and the cross, the flowers and the thorns that lacerated his head! Here, on Palm Sunday, they spread their garments before him; later they will take away Christ's garments in order to scourge him and nail him to the cross. Such is the limitation of this world, such the shortness of passing joy. The wise man showed his experience when he said: *Joy ends in grief*; and elsewhere: *Laughter I counted error, and to mirth I said: "Why are you deceived to no purpose?"* It was not inconsistent that our Lord should have wept amid these songs: *When he saw the city, he wept over it.* For he knew the inconstancy of those who were honoring him with garments and branches and songs. He knew also how many were being undermined and destroyed by worldly honors, as Solomon had said: *Prosperity will destroy the foolish.* This was utterly clear in the case of Antiochus, Herod, Saul, and many others. Therefore the prophet did not remain silent but said: *A thousand shall fall at your side*, that is, a few will fall away due to tribulation, and *ten thousand at your right hand*, that is, many more will be hurled down into sin by prosperity and honor, and will perish.

As for ourselves, we are the daughters of Zion and we dwell in the watch-tower and ark of the holy faith. Let us find our joy in Christ, our King, and not in worldly things that vanish like smoke. Isaiah urges us: *Behold our king, and his reward with him.* He comes for our sake, not for his own, and desires to enrich us with spiritual wealth and treasures. He came in gentleness, though formerly he roared like a lion and slew sinners with sword and fire and by opening the earth to swallow them. He came sitting on an ass and did not make his journey in a carriage or on a brightly outfitted horse, for he loves only poverty and does not require any tributes. He wishes to act as Savior and not to exercise rule like the princes of the earth, for his *kingdom is not of this world*.

Let us therefore immediately rise up and honor him as he deserves with garments and palm branches and songs of praise; let us sing *Hosanna to the Son of David* with heart and voice. He will certainly save us from the tyranny of Satan and grant us an outstanding freedom and his grace during this mortal life. And after this life is finished he will bestow heavenly glory on us. To him honor through all ages with the Father and the Paraclete. Amen.

(Palm Sunday, Sermon 22: *Opera Omnia* I, 430-431)

Alonso de Orozco, O.S.A. (1500-1591) studied at the University of Salamanca before entering the Augustinian novitiate there. His main apostolates in the Order were preaching and writing, and although he was chosen as royal preacher at the Spanish court, he preferred to speak to poor and simple people. His religious life was marked by a spirit of fraternity, gospel simplicity, and moderation in speech. As an ascetic and great mystic, he suffered crisis and spiritual aridity from 1522 to 1551. He was beatified by Pope Leo XIII in 1882.

Easter Triduum
Evening Mass of the Lord's Supper

Gospel: John 13:1-15

Before the feast of the Passover, Jesus realized that the hour had come for him to pass from this world to the Father. He had loved his own in this world, and would show his love for them to the end.

Commentary: L. de León

Jesus is the bread of life, as he calls himself, and this bread has been made out of two substances, holiness, which makes us strong, and hard work, which purges and destroys our vices. This bread has been kneaded with poverty, with humility, suffering, anguish, insults, blows, thorns, the cross, death. Each ingredient is a remedy against a vice. Still other ingredients are God's grace, the wisdom of the heavens, holy justice, moral values, and all the other gifts from the Holy Spirit. With such ingredients it becomes a powerful life-giving medicine which, eaten with faith, uproots and destroys our vices with its bitter parts, and enhances our life with its holy ingredients. The thorns in it purge us from our pride. The whippings in it cleanse us from excessive softness and love of pleasure. The cross fights selfishness, Christ's death puts an end to my vices, while other ingredients are equally active: When we eat in this bread God's justice, the spirit of justice grows in our soul. Holiness and grace act upon our body creating in us true holiness and grace. A portion of heaven is thus born in me when I become the son of God by eating in the bread the substance of God made man. We become then like him, dead to sin, living for justice, and true salvation, true Jesus, comes to us.

Jesus means therefore all kinds of salvation, because Jesus is a being entirely made of the essence of salvation. His words increase our health, and so do his works, his life, even his death. What he did, what he thought, what he suffered, his afterlife, everything connected with him gives us health and salvation. He heals us with his life experience, he gives us health and salvation through his experience with death. His grief and his pains diminish ours. Isaiah puts it briefly: *But he was wounded for our transgressions, he was bruised for our iniquities: The chastisement of our peace was upon him; and with his stripes we are healed.* His blisters are an ointment for our souls, his poured blood makes our virtue stronger. His example, as a model, wakes us up to purity, health, survival.

He is like the tree described in the Apocalypse, a tree planted on either side of the river, a tree of life, near the pure water of life, proceeding out of the throne of God and of the lamb. The leaves of the tree, it is written, were for the healing of nations. Thus Jesus: Not one leaf in his tree that is not a source of life, for me, for us, for the nations and for the whole world.

The tree of life described by Saint John bore twelve manner of fruits, and yielded one fruit every month. Again the parallel applies, for Jesus brings us health not by healing one illness or by helping us during one season of the year but by protecting us against every serious accident, every mortal wound, every bleeding cancer. He heals our pride by showing us his reed as a scepter. The purple cloak, given to him as an insult, can heal our ambition. His crown of thorns upon his head can heal our wicked love of empty pleasures. His bruised body wounded by the whip can get us rid of everything that is gross and clumsy. His nakedness reminds us that our cupidity is wrong. His endurance tells us that we should not be rash. Our self-centered attitude weakens when we remember how he never put himself in first place.

(*The Names of Christ* III, 362-364)

Luis de León, O.S.A. (1528-1591), after his education in Madrid and Valladolid, became an Augustinian friar in Salamanca in 1543. He was a great linguist and scholar, and held various chairs at the university there. His understanding of Hebrew led him to question the accuracy of the Vulgate, which made him suspect to the Inquisition. His translation of the Song of Songs from the Hebrew into Spanish led to his imprisonment for four years. He was eventually absolved and restored to his chair in the University. He wrote much poetry, but his best known prose work was *The Names of Christ*. Made up of commentaries on the different names of Christ — Shepherd, Prince of Peace, etc. — it is a beautifully written manual of Christianity.

Good Friday

Gospel: John 18:1-19.42   The passion of our Lord Jesus Christ.

Commentary: J. Metz

Have we really understood the impoverishment that Christ endured? Everything was taken from him during the passion, even the love that drove him to the cross. No longer did he savor his own love, no longer did he feel any spark of enthusiasm. His heart gave out and a feeling of utter helplessness came over him. Truly, he emptied himself. God's merciful hand no longer sustained him. His countenance was hidden during the passion, and Christ gaped into the darkness of nothingness and abandonment where God seemed to be no longer present. The Son of Man reached his destiny, stretched taut between a despising earth that had rejected him and a faceless heaven thundering God's "no" to sinful humankind. Jesus paid the price of futility. He became utterly poor.

In this total renunciation, however, Jesus perfected and proclaimed in action what took place in the depths of his being: he professed and accepted our humanity, he took on and endured our lot, he stepped down from his divinity. He came to us where we really are — with all our broken dreams and lost hopes, with the meaning of existence slipping through our fingers. He came and stood with us, struggling with his whole heart to have us say "yes" to our innate poverty.

God's fidelity to us is what gives us the courage to be true to ourselves. And the legacy of his total commitment to humankind, the proof of his fidelity to our poverty, is the cross. The cross is the sacrament of poverty of spirit, the sacrament of authentic humanness in a sinful world. It is the sign that one man remained true to his humanity, that he accepted it in full obedience.

Hanging in utter weakness on the cross, Christ revealed the divine meaning of human existence. It said something for the Jews and pagans that they found the cross scandalous and foolish. To the enlightened humanitarians and liberals of a later day the cross provokes only flat irony or weary skepticism. These self-styled advocates of humanity are more experienced; they are too indifferent to find the cross scandalous, yet not so naive to laugh at its foolishness. And what is it to us? Well, no one is exempted from the poverty of the cross; there is no guarantee against its intrusion. The antipathy to it found its way into the very midst of Christ's disciples: *You will all fall away because of me this night.*

Judas' betrayal may have been the result of frenzied impatience with Jesus' poverty, or a futile attempt to pressure Jesus into using his divine resources instead of accepting human impotence. In any case, it is not an isolated instance. Poverty of spirit is always betrayed most by those who are closest to it. It is the disciples of Christ in the Church who criticize and subvert it most savagely.

Perhaps that is why Jesus related the parable of the wheat grain. Finding in it a lesson for himself, he passed it on to his Church, so that she might remember it down through the ages, especially when the poverty intrinsic to human existence became repugnant: *Unless a grain of wheat falls into the earth and dies, it remains alone; but if it dies, it bears much fruit.*

(*Poverty of Spirit*, 18-20)

Johannes Baptist Metz (1928-) was born in Welluck, Germany, and ordained a priest in 1954. He studied at the University of Innsbruck and the University of Munich. He was professor of fundamental theology at the University of Münster. He has published many books and articles.

Easter Vigil

Gospel: Mark 16:1-8

When the Sabbath was over, Mary Magdalene, Mary the mother of James, and Salome bought perfumed oils with which they intended to go and anoint Jesus.

Commentary: L. Bouyer

The holy vigils, mentioned first in the Acts and still observed in the Church, are then more than a pious preparation for a passing feast. They give expression to that attitude of hopeful waiting characteristic of the Church. Inspired by the Holy Spirit whose pledge we have received, we look forward to the eucharistic banquet, and to the nuptial feast where the Bride and Bridegroom will be joined, not for a fleeting hour, under a veil of symbols that hide what they actually disclose, but in the full light of glory of a day that will last eternally.

Thus the first Christians used to gather at nightfall for their vigil, saying to one another, "The Lord is night." They always began this observance in the conviction that the Lord was going to appear with the first rays of morning; and the miracle is that this expectation, ever renewed, was never disappointed. Every time, at the bread-taking that closed the vigil, they recognized the One whom they loved without yet seeing Him: in the sacramental mystery, grace, after the manner of faith, revealed dimly the substance of gifts which the light of glory would soon illumine. With the Paraclete whispering in the depths of their ears, "Come to the Father," these pilgrims could resume with fresh enthusiasm their long journey toward the house of God, where the supper of His Son was prepared for them. Had not this Son Himself first come to their abodes? According to His promise, had He not eaten with them and they with Him? Christ-bearers, God bearers, these travelers possessed henceforth as viaticum, on their journey as exiles, the very One they awaited as recompense in their fatherland.

Such is the attitude the Church must foster in her members throughout the ages: a firm hope of the future as yet deferred but always imminent; a future very near indeed, for the past is a pledge of it and the present is sustained by anticipation of it. The Church maintains her members in that attitude chiefly by her liturgical vigils, whose uninterrupted tradition she has preserved from the Church of Jerusalem, from Christ Himself, and from the early prophets. If we wish to relive with her and her members those great sacred acts of the paschal triduum, which are her whole life, promised and possessed, we must begin by joining her in her watchful expectation.

(The Paschal Mystery, 4-5)

Louis Bouyer (1913-), born of Protestant parents, became a Lutheran minister until, as he says, "his profound studies into the nature of Protestantism as a genuinely spiritual movement led him gradually to the recognition that Catholicism was the only Church in which the positive elements of the Reformation could be exercised." He became a priest of the French Oratory and professor of spiritual theology at the Institut Catholique in Paris. He has written extensively on both ecumenism and liturgy.

Easter Sunday

Gospel: John 20:1-9

Early in the morning on the first day of the week, while it was still dark, Mary Magdalene came to the tomb.

Commentary: J. Daniélou

The resurrection means that here and now our humanity is elevated to the inaccessible realm of the divine. The resurrection is the Good News par excellence, the glorious destiny, far above its own nature, to which the Father's love has called the human race in his only Son through the gift of the Spirit. It is that unprecedented event by means of which we creatures of flesh and blood, so close to the animal world, are plunged alive into the consuming fire of God's triune life. Destroying everything mortal in us, that fire imparts incorruptibility *in order that what is mortal may be swallowed up by life*.

All this is only possible through the action of God. In Christ God comes down to us, takes our carnal nature, and raises it above itself in order to carry it into the intimate presence of the Father, *where Christ is seated at the right hand of God*.

Thus the resurrection of Christ constitutes the firstfruits of our own resurrection. With Christ part of our humanity is already taken up into the abyss of the Godhead. According to the metaphor employed by the writer to the Hebrews, Christ is like an anchor which instead of being let down into the depths of the sea is cast up into the heights of heaven. His is the guarantee of our hope, because that hope has already been fulfilled in him. What is more, in virtue of a mysterious force of gravity which Saint Augustine calls the *pondus ad sursum*, the glorified Christ draws the whole of humanity upward. *When I am lifted up from the earth*, Jesus said, *I shall draw all things to myself*.

Christ, the firstborn from the dead, was the first to break through the bounds of our enclosed, prison-like existence — a prison which can be enlarged by science, but from which science can never release us. It is through Christ that our destiny opens out into the infinite dimensions of the divine life.

The power of Christ's resurrection impinges upon our entire being. One day it will affect our dead bodies; a spark will flash out from it and touch them. It will raise them up to new life, no longer the life of mere flesh and blood but the life of the immortal Spirit who will communicate his own incorruptibility to our mortal bodies. But our soul experiences the power of the resurrection even now. When we are dead through the sin that deprives us of the divine life, our souls are touched by the risen life of Christ who revives the life of the Spirit in us. The Holy Spirit converts and strengthens our minds and hearts, filling them with his own life and empowering them to know and love the things of God. This we are enabled to do by means of a mysterious sharing in the knowledge and love with which God knows and loves himself.

(*La résurrection*, 135-138)

Jean Daniélou (1905-1974), born into a privileged family, his father being a politician and his mother an educationalist, did brilliantly at his studies, and in 1929 entered the Society of Jesus. He came under the influence of de Lubac and got to know Teilhard de Chardin. In 1940 he was chaplain to students in Paris and committed to the cause of resistance. Widely ecumenical in his views, he was a peritus at Vatican II under Pope John XXIII, and was made a cardinal by Pope Paul VI. As an author he was at home in many fields of erudition, including scripture, patristics, theology, and spirituality.

Second Sunday of Easter

Gospel: John 20:19-31

On the evening of that first day of the week, even though the disciples had locked the doors of the place where they were for fear of the Jews, Jesus came and stood before them.

Commentary: K. Adam

The initial, immediate reaction which the appearance of the risen Christ called forth among the apostles was the new and revolutionary realization that he truly was the Lord! *The Lord is risen indeed, and has appeared to Simon!* the eleven called out to the two disciples on their return from Emmaus. *It is the Lord!* John shouted when he saw the risen Christ on the shores of the lake. *My Lord and my God,* Thomas exclaimed when he saw the marks of the wounds in the risen Christ. *Lord, who are you?* asked Paul on the way to Damascus.

This "Kyrie-Lord" was the initial response of the new faith to the Easter message. In his first sermon at Pentecost, Peter declared solemnly, *Therefore let the whole house of Israel know for certain that God has made that same Jesus, whom you crucified, both Lord and Christ.*

According to Jewish and Hellenistic linguistic usage, "the Lord-kyrios" is God revealing himself to his people in might. If the apostles had seen Jesus more as a man before their Easter experience, and realized his divinity only when it broke through the surface of his humanity in signs and words, afterward that divinity became the central fact of their belief in the risen Christ in their midst, and they were aware of his humanity only in relationship to this divinity. The experience of Easter gave an important depth and clarity to the apostles' concept of Christ. The old ideas of the human figure of Jesus were incorporated into and permeated by the new concept of his divinity. For the first time they were intuitively certain that Jesus the man was, in the depth of his being, their "Lord and God"; and because it was the Lord himself who stood before them in human form, their other ideas began to clarify. They realized that his proper place, his original homeland, could be nowhere else but in heaven at the right hand of the Father.

The Risen One himself assured them, *I ascend to my Father, and your Father, to my God, and your God.* This is why the apostles now joyfully preach the news that *God has exalted Jesus to his right hand.* Never again will this "seated at the right hand of the Father" be absent from the Christian creed.

The natural consequence was that from this risen Lord seated at the right hand of the Father, all life and spirit, all grace and forgiveness, all power and might should be poured out over all his people. Again and again the apostles hear such words from the risen Christ, *Lo, I am with you always, even to the end of the world,* and *Behold I send you my Spirit which the Father promised,* and *Receive the Holy Spirit. If you forgive the sins of any, they are forgiven; if you retain them, they are retained.*

The power of the risen Christ extended not only to the heights of the spirit but to the very roots of all being, there where life itself wells up from a thousand springs, and when death lurks. The most sweeping, thrilling realization which impressed itself on the consciousness of the disciples was that in the new life of their risen Lord they were sure of their own eternal life. The resurrection of the Lord was a truly cosmic event for them, because it guaranteed not only their own resurrection, but the raising of the dead of the whole earth.

(*Jesus Christus*, 234-236)

Karl Adam (1876-1966) was born in Bavaria, studied for the priesthood and was ordained in 1900. After some experience of pastoral work he taught first at the University of Munich and in 1918 became a professor at Strasbourg. A year later he was appointed to the chair of dogmatic theology at Tübingen, which he held until 1949. He was among the forerunners of ecumenism, liberal and up to date in thought, but always orthodox. His writings, which had great influence especially on the laity, include: *The Nature of Catholicism, Christ Our Brother,* and *The Son of God.*

Third Sunday of Easter

Gospel: Luke 24:35-48

The disciples recounted what had happened on the road to Emmaus and how they had come to know Jesus in the breaking of bread. While they were still speaking about all this, he himself stood in their midst.

Commentary: M. D'Arcy

The disciples of Christ were changed from despair to unshakable joy by the events of Easter. Human beings differ in temperament, and there are those who would have us believe we cannot change our humors. It is true that one who "sucks melancholy out of a song as a weasel sucks eggs" cannot be like the laughing cavalier. But all can come to happiness and acquire a disposition in which hope and courage have the upper hand, and fear and depression are like "the snake beneath Michael's foot." Such a disposition, however, to be secure and to give real peace must rest on a profound conviction of truth. The apostles had lost heart after Gethsemane; and then they saw a dead man alive and speaking in their midst, and truth came upon them in such a way as never to be dislodged.

It was a strange truth, which looked unblinkingly at shame and suffering and death. Those once abject apostles now preached what they felt might be to others a stumbling block or folly, of a God crucified and risen, a Lamb slain and alive. They created hope out of death and were able to christen their wild-worst best.

The gospel narratives of the scenes after the resurrection have a sunlit beauty: the good women at the empty tomb; the two disciples walking to Emmaus; the breakfast at dawn by the lakeside. Saint Paul never saw Christ in the flesh, and yet he has the same conviction as those first witnesses. *If Christ be not risen from the dead we are the most miserable of men.* We are like Saint Paul in not having seen with our own eyes the wounds in the hands and feet of Christ; but like him we can grow a sure conviction that the man lifted up on his cross was truly the Son of God, and that God, who with majestic love reigns from a cross, continues to defeat evil and give life, and nothing man can do will thwart him.

(*Of God and Man*, 75-76)

Martin C. D'Arcy, S.J. (1888-1976) was born in Bath, England, and educated at Stonyhurst. He joined the Society of Jesus in 1906 and was ordained a priest in 1921. He read for a classical degree at Oxford (1912-1946), took a double first in Mods and Greats, and subsequently won the John Locke Scholarship for his essay on Greek moral philosophy. He taught at Oxford, wrote numerous books and articles, and traveled extensively. He died in London on 20 November 1976.

Fourth Sunday of Easter

Gospel: John 10:11-18

Jesus said: "I am the good shepherd; the good shepherd lays down his life for the sheep."

Commentary: L. de León

*J*esus is not only a shepherd, but he is a shepherd as no other has previously existed, which he expresses in relation to himself by saying, *I am the good shepherd*. In this phrase the word "good" marks excellence, as if to say he were "the best shepherd of all." His first superiority is that the other shepherds are such accidentally or by chance, while Christ is born to be a shepherd, and before birth he wished to be born for that, so that he descended from heaven and he became man-shepherd, as he himself says, to seek out man, the lost sheep. And since he was born to lead to pasture, it is to the shepherds that at the time of his birth he made his coming known. In addition to that, the other shepherds guard their flocks which they find, but our Shepherd constitutes himself the flock which he must protect. What we owe to Christ is not only that he governs us and makes us feed in the manner just spoken of; it is above all that we, who are savage animals, he transforms into sheep, that he goes to find the lost ones, and he infuses into us the spirit of simplicity, of sweetness, and of holy and faithful humility by which we belong to his flock.

His third superiority is that he died for the good of his flock, which no other shepherd did, and that he snatched us from the teeth of the wolf; he consented to offer himself as victim to the wolf. The fourth is that he is at the same time shepherd and pasture and that in feeding his sheep he gives himself to them. To govern his own and to lead them to pasture, Christ did no other thing than to place himself among them, to permeate himself with them, incorporate their life in himself and in the warmth of this faithful love, make his sheep go through his entrails in such a way that once gone through he transforms his sheep into himself. They feed themselves from him, removing themselves from themselves and taking upon themselves the qualities of Christ. The flock grows,

58

thanks to his happy pasture, and slowly they become one with its Shepherd. Finally, if other names and offices are fitting for Christ, either from some beginning, or for a certain end, or during some period or time, this name of Shepherd is endless because, before being born in the flesh, he nourished creatures as soon as they appeared; because he governed and conserved things, he himself fed the angels and *These wait all upon you, that you may give them their meat in due season*. In reality, after his birth as man he feeds men from his spirit and flesh. As soon as he ascended to heaven, he made his nourishment rain upon the earth. Then and now and later, in all time and at every hour, he nourishes men in a thousand secretive and marvelous ways. On earth he feeds them, and in heaven he will also be their Shepherd when he will lead them there; then the centuries will be consumed, and insofar as his sheep will live, they will live eternally with him; he will live in them, communicating his own life to them, having become their shepherd and their pasture.

(*The Names of Christ* I, 102-103)

Luis de León, O.S.A. (1528-1591), after his education in Madrid and Valladolid, became an Augustinian friar in Salamanca in 1543. He was a great linguist and scholar, and held various chairs at the university there. His understanding of Hebrew led him to question the accuracy of the Vulgate, which made him suspect to the Inquisition. His translation of the Song of Songs from the Hebrew into Spanish led to his imprisonment for four years. He was eventually absolved and restored to his chair in the University. He wrote much poetry, but his best known prose work was *The Names of Christ*. Made up of commentaries on the different names of Christ — Shepherd, Prince of Peace, etc. — it is a beautifully written manual of Christianity.

Fifth Sunday of Easter

Gospel: John 15:1-8

Jesus said to his disciples: "I am the true vine and my Father is the vinegrower."

Commentary: L. Bouyer

The symbol of the vine was well known to the Jews. It appears frequently in the Old Testament to designate the People of God, and to depict the loving care with which he surrounded them. Jesus uses it in the same sense in the synoptics. But in Saint John's gospel, by identifying himself with the true vine, Jesus proclaims that the true Israel is in him, and only those united with him can form a part of it. Yet even this is not enough: we must note that the prophets by the term "vine" usually meant "vineyard." Hence we are not speaking of a single vine-stock; the simile is condensed the better to convey the idea of unity in love.

Jesus here intends to declare that he is not only united to his disciples, but is one with them. He is not only the source of their life; they can only live by being integrated into his being to the extent of forming one single organism with him. Here it may be said that Jesus is no longer considering himself as an individual, but as a living "collective" which is yet a perfect unity; that he compromises in himself all regenerate humanity. This corresponds to the Pauline doctrine of the Church as Christ's mystical body. Jesus and his members are not two entities any more than the head and the body are. But the parable of the vine expresses an even more profound assimilation. When Jesus says *I am the true vine*, there is no question of the two complementary elements, but of one divine Person extending his incarnation from the main stem, Jesus the man, into the branches. He is the living principle of unity for the whole, constituting, according to Augustine's magnificent phrase, "the whole Christ," head and members.

It is only through Jesus that the vine can thrust its roots into the depths of divine life, yet this life of God does really find its way to the extremities of the farthest branches. Jesus is the source, but the branches must draw from the life-springs in him. Here we have two statements about the branches: first, that they cannot bear fruit apart from Christ, so that they must remain organically united with him. This says under a different figure, but in the same eucharistic context, what our Lord had already expressed by the words: *Unless you eat my flesh and drink my blood you can have no life in yourselves.* Secondly, the branches, even though they are in Christ, have to bear fruit or they will be cut off from the stock. Believers grafted into Christ, pulsing with the grace of the vital union, are purged, "pruned" by God, to make their fruitfulness ever more abundant. On the contrary, one who is closed against the life-giving action of the sap must be removed from the stock, and burnt. Christ's offshoots must bear fruit or they will be condemned to the flames, but their fruit springs entirely from their union with Christ; it is his fruit.

What is this fruit? The organic unity between Christ and his own has but one fruit, the union of love. His whole purpose in becoming incarnate was to establish his disciples in his love, as he is in his Father's love. It is by obedience that he remains in the love of the Father, and it is by obedience also that his followers remain in his love.

(*Le quatrième Evangile*, 203-205)

Louis Bouyer (1913-), born of Protestant parents, became a Lutheran minister until, as he says, "his profound studies into the nature of Protestantism as a genuinely spiritual movement led him gradually to the recognition that Catholicism was the only Church in which the positive elements of the Reformation could be exercised." He became a priest of the French Oratory and professor of spiritual theology at the Institut Catholique in Paris. He has written extensively on both ecumenism and liturgy.

Sixth Sunday of Easter

Gospel: John 15:9-17 — Jesus said to his disciples: "As the Father has loved me, so I have loved you. Live on in my love."

Commentary: M. Delbrêl

My little children, you must truly love one another sums up all that the aged Saint John had to say.

It is God whom we love. Love of God is the first commandment, but the second is like it; that is to say it is only through others that we can return God's love for us. The danger is that the second commandment may become the first. However, we have a way to check this, which is to love each person as if he or she were Christ, to love God in every human being, without preference, distinction, or exception.

The second danger is that we may find love impossible, and that is sure to happen if we separate love from faith and hope. It is prayer that gives us faith and hope. Without prayer we can never love. It is in prayer, and prayer alone, that Christ will reveal himself to us in each person we meet, by a faith that grows ever keener and more clear-sighted. It is in prayer that we can ask for the gift of loving each person, a grace without which there can be no love. It is through prayer that our hope will measure up to the stature or number of those we are destined to encounter or to the depth of their needs. It is the expansion of faith and hope by prayer that will clear the path before us of the most cumbersome obstruction to love, which is self-concern.

The third danger is that instead of loving *as Jesus loved us* we may love in a human fashion. This perhaps is the greatest of dangers, since human love, simply because it is love, is a beautiful and noble thing. Unbelievers may show a superb love for others. But we ourselves have not been called to that kind of love. It is not our own love that we have to give: it is the love of God — that love which is a divine Person. That love is God's gift to ourselves, but

62

it remains a gift which must as it were pass through us, bore a channel through us to find its way elsewhere and flow into others. It is a gift that claims sovereign power; we are not to trust in the power of anything else. It is something we may not keep to ourselves, or we risk its being extinguished and ceasing to be a gift.

(Le joie de croire, 71-71)

Madeleine Delbrêl (1904-1964), born in Dordogne, France, died in Paris. In her writings she emphasized the importance of sharing belief with those who do not believe and thus being open daily to the demands of the word of God.

Ascension

Gospel: Matthew 28:16-20   Jesus appeared to the Eleven and said to them: "Go into the whole world and proclaim the good news to all creation. The one who believes in it and accepts baptism will be saved."

Commentary: J. Corbon   **W**e can only wonder at, and try to recapture for ourselves, the insight shown by the early Christians and by Christians down to the beginning of the second millennium, who placed the Christ of the ascension in the dome of their churches. When the faithful gathered to manifest and become the body of Christ, they saw their Lord both as present and as coming. He is the head and draws his body toward the Father while giving it life through his Spirit. The iconography of the churches of both East and West during that period was as it were an extension of the mystery of the ascension throughout the entire visible church. Christ, *the Lord of all* (Pantocrator), is *the cornerstone which the builders had rejected*; when he is raised up on the cross, he is in fact being raised to the Father's side and, in his life-giving humanity, becomes with the Father the wellspring of the river of life. In the vault of the apses there was also to be seen the Woman and her Child; that single vision embraces both the Virgin who give birth and the Church in the wilderness. In the sanctuary were to be seen the angels of the ascension or other expressions of the theophanies of the Holy Spirit. Finally, on the walls of the church were the living stones: the throng of saints, the "cloud of the witnesses," the Church of the "firstborn." The ascension of the Lord was thus really the new space for the liturgy of the last times, and the iconography of the church built of stone was its transparent symbol.

In his ascension, then, Christ did not at all disappear; on the contrary, he began to appear and to come. For this reason, the hymns we use in our churches sing of him as "the Sun of justice" that rises in the east. He who is the splendor of the Father and who once descended into the depths of our darkness is now exalted and fills all things with his light. Our last times are located between that first ascension and the ascension that will carry him to the zenith of his glorious parousia. The Lord has not gone away to rest from his redemptive toil; his "work" continues, but now at the Father's side, and because he is there he is now much closer to us, "very near to us," in the work that is the liturgy of the last times. *He leads captives*, namely, us, to the new world of his resurrection and bestows his *gifts*, his Spirit, on human beings. His ascension is a progressive movement, *from beginning to beginning*.

Jesus is, of course, at his Father's side. If, however, we reduce this "ascent" to a particular moment in our mortal history, we simply forget that beginning with the hour of his cross and resurrection Jesus and the human race are henceforth one. He became a son of man in order that we might become children of God. The ascension is progressive *until we all...form the perfect Man fully mature with the fullness of Christ himself*. The movement of the ascension will be complete only when all the members of his body have been drawn to the Father and brought to life by his Spirit. Is that not the meaning of the answer the angels gave to the disciples: *Why are you Galileans standing here looking into the sky? This Jesus who has been taken up from you into heaven will come back in the same way as you have seen him go to heaven*. The ascension does not show us in advance the setting of the final parousia; it is rather the activation of the paschal energy of Christ *who fills all things*. It is the ever-new "moment" of his coming.

(*The Wellspring of Worship*, 36-37)

Jean Corbon is a member of the Dominican community of Beirut and author of the book *L'Église des Arabes*. His whole thrust in writing on liturgy is to rediscover its meaning and to understand how the whole of life finds itself transformed.

Seventh Sunday of Easter

Gospel: John 17:11-19

Jesus looked up to heaven and prayed: "O Father most holy, protect them with your name which you have given me, that they may be one, even as we are one."

Commentary: P. Bernard

To keep the disciples in the divine name, to lead them thus toward the divine unity, Jesus confesses that he had applied himself to this throughout the time that he had been with them. This avowal says a great deal, and not only about the sentiments of the Man-God, but also concerning the metaphysics of the incarnation. The Christ never ceased to envelop his own in the protection of God; he had made the divine presence more of a guardian for them; he had revealed to them the providence of God; he had exercised on their behalf this very providence. I have watched, he says to his Father, and not one of them has been lost, except, he interjects sadly, the child of perdition, he whose ruin you had foretold and who was, so to speak, lost in your thought. Only, he adds, I am returning now to you. And he leaves the phrase hanging, he does not finish the request, as if he was saying: Father, you know what you have to do; I am withdrawing from them the assistance which has rendered them sensitive to your presence, I withdraw it from them in order to go to you; it is for you to supply for their need, in doubling your providence in their regard, in devoting to them special attention.

As regards the separation from the world, Jesus does not ask that his disciples be taken out of this environment: they have to be present in the world, they have a mission to fulfill there. But he requests that they be preserved from the evil that reigns in the world, their role being to oppose this evil, to be the salt which prevents corruption, the light which shines in the darkness. One can also interpret evil not as a neuter but as a masculine: it designates then not evil but the evil one, the prince of this world, the devil who presides over the evil which is in the world. In the first Johannine epistle this evil one is an important and nefarious personage; but the fourth gospel does not seem to be so marked by this thought: there is question of evil works, but not precisely of the evil person who stirs them up. The preservation of the disciples represents the negative side of the sanctity which Jesus asks for them; the consecration which he defines next will be its positive side.

To sanctify is to consecrate. *Sanctify them in the truth*. Truth is a word of greatness in this place; and little is needed that it even be a divine name. Jesus prays that his disciples might be thoroughly transformed in the revelation of the truth and in the possession of the truth. This revelation, which comes from the Father, which is the Word of the Father, places them in the truth of God. Therefrom derives their great consecration: he who has his vision fixed upon God will know how to live in God and for God. The rest follows, but first let them be in the truth: such is the grace which Jesus wishes to his disciples. Their sanctification prepares them for their mission, the one and the other modeled on those of Jesus himself.

(The Mystery of Jesus, 334-335)

Pierre Bernard, O.P., a ranking French exegete and spiritual writer, has combined his talents in a justly heralded work about the Son of God: *The Mystery of Jesus*. Making use of the latest findings of modern scholarship together with a profound knowledge of human nature, the author has drawn a portrait of Jesus that has earned praise from critics and public alike; the work has been quickly translated into many other languages and has brought the mystery of Jesus home to countless modern readers.

Pentecost Sunday

Gospel: John 15:26-27; 16:12-15 Jesus said to his disciples: "When the Paraclete comes, the Spirit of truth who comes from the Father — and whom I myself will send from the Father — he will bear witness on my behalf."

Commentary: Paul VI

Only after the descent of the Holy Spirit on the day of Pentecost did the apostles set out for the ends of the earth to begin the great task of evangelization entrusted to the Church. This was interpreted by Saint Peter as the fulfillment of the prophecy of Joel: *I will pour out my Spirit on all flesh.* Peter was himself filled with the Holy Spirit for the very purpose of empowering him to proclaim publicly that Jesus was the Son of God. In the same way Paul was filled with the Spirit before he embarked on his apostolic ministry, while Stephen, being *a man full of the Holy Spirit,* was chosen for the ministry of service and later to bear witness in his own blood. Having made eloquent apostles of Peter, Paul, and the twelve and inspired them with the message they were to preach, the Spirit also fell upon those who listened to God's word.

The Church grows by being filled with the consoling presence of the Holy Spirit who is the principle of its life. He it is who enables believers to understand the mystery of Christ and his teaching. As the Spirit was active in the initial stages of the Church's existence, so now he is at work in each and every preacher of the gospel who is open to his guidance. He suggests to the minds of evangelists such words as he alone can inspire, at the same time disposing the hearts of their hearers to accept the gospel message and the proclamation of the kingdom.

Techniques of evangelization are of undoubted value, but even the best of these is no substitute for the hidden working of the Spirit. Without the Holy Spirit no amount of preparation and study on the part of the preacher is of any avail, and the clearest reasoning is powerless to persuade the human heart unless the Spirit has prompted it. Even the most perspicacious arguments based on sociology and psychology turn out to be worthless if the power of the Spirit does not accompany them.

That the present time is a privileged moment of the Spirit for the Church is a fact of which we are very conscious today. Everywhere believers are trying to know and understand the Spirit as he is revealed in the Scriptures. Unfurling their sails to catch his breath, they gladly entrust themselves to his guidance. People gather together in large numbers to pray, freely surrendering themselves to his action. Yet if the influence of the Holy Spirit is so great in the life of the Church at large, it is of paramount importance in the work of evangelization. It was no mere chance that the first steps in preaching the gospel were taken on the day of Pentecost at the inspiration of the Spirit of God.

From all this it is easy to see that the initiative in spreading the gospel belongs to the Holy Spirit. It is the Spirit who prompts the preacher and prepares the listener's heart to accept and understand the word of salvation. With equal reason the Holy Spirit can be called the goal of all evangelization, because it is he who brings the new creation into being. He alone fashions that new humanity which must be the aim of all evangelization, that unity in diversity which the preaching of the gospel in the Christian community necessarily calls forth. It is due to the Holy Spirit that the gospel permeates the world, since it is he who enables evangelists to read the God-given signs of the times and to explain their significance in the concrete circumstances of human life.

(*Evangelii nuntiandi*, 75)

Paul VI (1897-1978), born Giovanni Battista Montini, was ordained a priest in 1920 and in 1925 entered the Vatican Secretariat of State. In this service of the Church he filled several important posts until he was named archbishop of Milan by Pius XII on 1 November 1954. Montini was made a cardinal in December 1958, and elected pope on 21 June 1963. During his long pontificate he showed himself to be an intrepid pastor and a determined promoter of the decrees of the Second Vatican Council. In spite of opposition he firmly held the bark of Peter on its course into a new age.

Trinity Sunday

Gospel: Matthew 28:16-20   The eleven disciples made their way to Galilee, to the mountain to which he had summoned them. At the sight of him, those who had entertained doubts fell down in homage.

Commentary: Julian of Norwich

I saw the blessed Trinity working. I saw that there were these three attributes: fatherhood, motherhood, and lordship — all in one God. In the almighty Father we have been sustained and blessed with regard to our created natural being from before all time. By the skill and wisdom of the Second Person we are sustained, restored, and saved with regard to our sensual nature, for he is our Mother, brother, and Savior. In our good Lord the Holy Spirit we have, after our life and hardship is over, that reward and rest which surpasses forever any and everything we can possibly desire — such is his abounding grace and magnificent courtesy.

Our life too is threefold. In the first stage we have our being, in the second our growth, and in the third our perfection. The first is nature, the second mercy, and the third grace. For the first I realized that the great power of the Trinity is our Father, the deep wisdom our Mother, and the great love our Lord. All this we have by nature and in our created and essential being. Moreover I saw that the Second Person who is our Mother with regard to our essential nature, that same dear Person has become our Mother in the matter of our sensual nature. We are God's creation twice: essential being and sensual nature. Our being is that higher part which we have in our Father, God almighty, and the second Person of the Trinity is Mother of his basic nature, providing the substance in which we are rooted and grounded. But he is our Mother also in mercy, since he has taken our sensual nature upon himself. Thus "our Mother" describes the different ways in which he works, ways which are separate to us, but held together in him. In our Mother, Christ, we grow and develop; in his mercy he reforms and restores us; through his passion, death, and resurrection he has united us to our being. So does our Mother work in mercy for all his children who respond to him and obey him.

Grace works with mercy too, and especially in two ways. The work is that of the Third Person, the Holy Spirit, who works by *rewarding* and *giving*. Rewarding is the generous gift of truth that the Lord makes to him who has suffered. Giving is a magnanimous gesture which he makes freely by his grace: perfect, and far beyond the desserts of any of his creatures.

(*Revelations of Divine Love*, 165-166)

Julian, an anchoress who lived in solitude in Norwich, England, in the late fourteenth century, received the sixteen "showings" or revelations of God's love in a series of experienced visions. Julian's writings reveal a person who experienced God directly and not self-consciously as "our mother." Her revelations of the feminine side of God represent a significant contribution to the tradition. Her graphic visions of the humanity of Christ are marked by vivid imagery and detail. But the special appeal of Julian lies in her theology of the all-embracing fullness of divine love.

Corpus Christi

Gospel: Mark 14:12-16.22-26 On the first day of Unleavened Bread, when it was customary to sacrifice the paschal lamb, the disciples said to Jesus, "Where do you wish us to go to prepare the Passover supper for you?"

Commentary: Hildegard of Bingen

When the Son of God celebrated with his disciples that consummation by which he was to pass out of the world, no longer, as before, living among the events of the world but enduring the Passion of the cross in accordance with his Father's will, with supreme devotion he took the bread in remembrance of his body for human salvation. With all his longing he reminded his Father how he came forth from him and wanted to return to him, and prayed him to consider whether it was possible, because of the weakness of his flesh, for the chalice he was to drink to pass from him; but this was not to happen. And therefore he blessed that bread in remembrance of the sweat of his body; for in the anguish of his Passion, as he submitted to his Father's command and was willing to die on the cross, he gave his body and blood to his disciples, so that they would not forget his example.

And he broke it for them; for that passion was hard for his body to bear. But nonetheless he obeyed his Father and conquered cruel death by the death of his body; and so he showed that his body and blood were also to be given to believers in him in the mystery of the oblation.

And he gave it to his disciples for true salvation, that they too might do such things in his name as he was doing for love of them; thus he was saying in a gentle voice, "You who humbly wish to follow me, take with ardent love this example I leave you, my passion and my works I have done at my Father's command, when he sent me to teach and to manifest his kingdom; and eat faithfully what I give you, for it is my body." What does this mean? "Eat my body, for you must imitate my works in your spirits and your flesh, whenever the Holy Spirit inspires them in your hearts, as a person swallows the food he is sending to his stomach; as you and all who wish to keep my precepts should follow me in my works, so too you should eat my body."

And then the Son of God, taking for salvation the saving cup, gave thanks to his Father; for when the blood poured out from his side, grace was given to believers that was so strong that it conquered the ancient serpent, delivered lost humanity and strengthened the whole Church in faith. How? The Savior in the sweetness of his love gave his precious example to all his faithful, summoning them with gentle inspiration by saying, "Drink with confidence from this saving cup, all you who desire to follow me faithfully, that for love of me you may chastise your bodies by privation and restrain your blood by toil, and deny yourselves to strengthen the Church; even as I submitted myself to the Passion, and shed my blood for your redemption, not thinking of the tenderness of my flesh but thirsting for your salvation. For this blood, which is shed for you, is not that blood of the Old Testament, which was shed in shadow, but my blood of the New Testament, which was given for the salvation of the peoples. How? I who am the only-born of my mother, the Son of the most pure Virgin, shed my blood on the cross to redeem people who contemplate me by faith. And as I then gave it for the deliverance of the human race, so now I give it on the altar for humanity, to cleanse those who faithfully receive it."

(*Scivias*, 249-250)

Hildegard of Bingen (1098-1179) was a German nun, mystic, and scholar. Having entered religious life as a child, Hildegard founded the Benedictine convent of Rupertberg near Bingen in 1147. Renowned for her visions, related in the *Scivias*, Hildegard was a theologian, physician, and composer as well as an energetic reformer.

Sacred Heart

Gospel: John 19:31-37

Since it was the Preparation Day the Jews did not want to have the bodies left on the cross during the sabbath, for that sabbath was a solemn feast day.

Commentary: Pius XII

*T*he most sacred heart of Jesus participated in the closest possible way in the life of the incarnate Word. To this same degree his heart, no less than the other elements of his human nature, was assumed as the instrument of the Godhead for carrying out the works of divine grace and almighty power. There can be no doubt, therefore, that his heart is an appropriate symbol of that immense love which moved our Savior to pour out his blood and thus enter into mystical marriage with the Church. "Out of charity he suffered for the sake of the Church, which was to be united to him as his bride," says Saint Thomas Aquinas.

From the wounded heart of the Redeemer, then, the Church was born to dispense the blood of the redemption. From that same heart has sprung in great profusion the grace of the sacraments, whence the children of the Church draw supernatural life. So we read in the sacred liturgy: "From that heart by spear-point severed the Church is born, Bride of Christ" and again, "Praise be to your heart, Lord Jesus, font of grace for humankind."

Echoing the voices of the ancient Fathers and writers of the Church, to whom this symbolism was familiar, Saint Thomas explains: "From Christ's side there flowed water to wash us and blood to redeem us. Thus the blood stands for the sacrament of the eucharist, while the water corresponds to the sacrament of baptism. Baptism, however, derives its cleansing property from the power of Christ's blood."

What is here written of Christ's side, wounded and laid open by the soldier, is to be affirmed of his heart, which was certainly reached by the blow of the spear; this we know because the soldier drove home his spear precisely in order to make sure that the crucified Christ was dead. Hence the wound made in the most sacred heart of Jesus at the moment when he had done with this mortal life has been all down the ages a vivid image of the freely bestowed love by which God gave his only Son to redeem the human race, and by which Christ loved us all so intensely that he immolated himself as a blood-soaked victim on Calvary for our sake. *Christ loved us and delivered himself for us as a sacrificial offering to God in fragrant sweetness.*

Since our Savior has ascended to heaven in his body adorned with the brightness of eternal glory, and taken his seat at the Father's right hand, he has never ceased to pursue his bride, the Church, with the burning love that throbs in his heart. In his hands, feet, and side he bears the shining marks of his wounds, tokens of the threefold victory he has won over the devil, sin, and death. In the same way he bears in his heart, laid up as in a precious casket, those unlimited treasures of merit which are the spoils of his triple triumph, and he bestows them plentifully on redeemed humanity. This is a truth full of encouragement for us, vouched for by the apostle when he says: *Ascending on high Christ led captivity captive, and gave gifts to the human race.* He who descended is none other than he who has ascended above the highest heavens to fill all creation.

(*Haurietis aquas*: AAS 48 [1956] 333-334)

Pius XII (1876-1958), born Eugenio Pacelli at Rome, became a priest and served in the Church's diplomatic corps until his election to the papacy in 1939 under the name Pius XII. There was scarcely any field of human knowledge in which this dedicated man of God did not bring to bear the witness of the gospel. Encyclical Letters, speeches to scholars, workers, married people, and the like — these made him a veritable encyclopedic pope. His encyclicals on Scripture (*Divino afflante Spiritu*), the Church (*Mystici Corporis*), and liturgical theology (*Mediator Dei*) heavily influenced the life of the Church and paved the way for the Second Vatican Council.

Second Sunday in Ordinary Time

Gospel: John 1:35-42

John was in Bethany across the Jordan with two of his disciples. As he watched Jesus walk by he said, "Look! There is the Lamb of God!"

Commentary: D. Dumm

*I*n John's version of the call of the first disciples, we read that two of them were following Jesus. *When he turned and saw them following him, he asked "What are you looking for?" They said, "Rabbi" (which means a teacher), "where are you staying?" "Come and see," he replied.* In view of John's love for symbolism, it would be a mistake to see this simply as a friendly exchange. Rather, the question of Jesus implies that he perceives in them (and in us) that deep longing that is characteristic of humans when they allow themselves to be in touch with their true condition. It is as if he had said, "Why, you must be earthlings, for I see that you are searching for something!" The disciples call him "Rabbi" because they sense that if he knows their innermost yearning, he must also know where to find what they seek; he must be a teacher of truth. So they ask him, *Where are you staying?* They are certainly not asking him for his address. Their question means, "Where can we find you and learn from you about our true home? Jesus says, in reply, *Come and see*. He does not give a pat answer; he offers instead an invitation to walk with him and to learn what living in hope means, what the journey means — to learn of its pain but also of its joy, and most of all of its happy ending, its true homecoming.

This ability to live in hope may very well be the single most distinctive characteristic of the biblical person as opposed to the devotee of secular philosophy. From the secular perspective, everything must make sense here and now; human success and happiness must be found in this life. Hence the need to seek immediate fulfillment. Time is an enemy, especially as one grows older, for it erodes relentlessly the opportunity for present enjoyment. From the biblical perspective, it is promise that dominates and true fulfillment is reserved for the end of life. The only real concern during life is to assure that one has chosen the path that leads to that homeland. This is not an easy path; it puts aside personal gratification for the good of others; it is the Jesus-path of loving care and sacrifice. From this perspective, the length of life is not a major concern because one step in the right direction is as good as a thousand. This provides freedom from excessive anxiety or angry frustration; it also means an old age that is not just meaningless and helpless waiting for death but rather joyful expectation as one looks forward eagerly for the arrival at home. The fact that perhaps only a few can claim this experience is simply proof that we need to be more fully converted from the infection of secular philosophy to the bright hope of biblical revelation.

(Flowers in the Desert, a Spirituality of the Bible, 60-61)

Demetrius Dumm, O.S.B., is professor of New Testament at Saint Vincent Seminary in Latrobe, PA. Having studied at the École Biblique in Jerusalem and the Pontifical Biblical Commission in Rome, Father Dumm has also been a faculty member at the Institute of Formative Spirituality at Duquesne University and in the Intercommunity Program for Women Religious in southwestern Pennsylvania.

Third Sunday in Ordinary Time

Gospel: Mark 1:14-20

After John's arrest, Jesus appeared in Galilee proclaiming God's good news: "This is the time of fulfillment. The reign of God is at hand! Reform your lives and believe in the good news!"

Commentary: J. L. Bernardin

Reform your lives and believe in the gospel! With these words Jesus began his public ministry. Once we have heard the good news, what is left to do but to pay the price of it — to sell all to possess a pearl of such great worth? To respond means to change in mind and heart. It means faith and love. It means a new mind illumined by faith and a new heart inflamed by love of Jesus Christ.

Prayer leads us ultimately to make radical demands on ourselves. One's personality, understood as a complex pattern of attitudes and values, must be dismantled and reassembled according to the mind of Christ Jesus. One's attitudes toward fame, position, power, wealth, family ties, marriage, must be radically examined in the blinding light of the gospel. No one who encounters the Light of the world in the scriptures can respond otherwise than by the prayer which humbly begs for the mind of Christ.

All prayer involves our hearts. Where a person's treasure is, Jesus said, there is his heart. To reject Satan and false goods for the treasure of Jesus Christ is to experience a change of heart. The heart rooted in Christ prayfully cries out its allegiance.

New love in Christ is not without pain. Prayer involving *metanoia* or conversion requires "a deep change of heart in which we die on a certain level of our being in order to find ourselves alive and free on another, more spiritual level." Prayer consisting of this kind of loving response transforms us into "new people" in Christ.

I have described prayer as an inspired response to an ever-present God *reconciling the world to himself in Christ*. Others describe prayer as humanity's inspired, conscious effort to seek union with God. However described, prayer unites us with God. Thus prayer is more than a means; it is an end.

In this life all union with God, every response to the God who seeks us, and every seeking of God are incomplete and imperfect. Humankind cannot perfectly possess God. Nor can God, because of humanity's sinfulness, completely be at one with any one of us. Though Mary was sinless, even she was not perfectly one with God in the face-to-face encounter we all long for.

But at the same time, paradoxically, we know that if we hunger and thirst for God we do have communion — imperfect but real — with him now. God is within us and we are at one with God if, like the apostle Paul, we take up discipleship with the ardent longing of being dissolved into the Lord.

Who would not risk discipleship even unto death to be with God?

All our prayers of petition should be related to the desire for that perfect love, peace, and joy that come from being with God. Our faith that God revealed himself as a Savior in the past is the basis for our confident hope in his mercies yet to come. We pray for our present needs in the light of "one great act of giving birth"; for we, as firstfruits of the Holy Spirit, and all creation groan as we wait for our bodies to be set free.

(Prayer in Our Time)

Joseph Bernardin (1928-), born at Columbia, South Carolina, was educated at St. Mary's Seminary, Baltimore, and The Catholic University of America. Ordained in 1952, he served as vicar general of the Charleston diocese and then became auxiliary bishop of Atlanta in 1966. In 1968 he was named general secretary of the United States Catholic Conference and later archbishop of Cincinnati. In 1982 he was named archbishop of Chicago and elevated as a cardinal in 1983.

Fourth Sunday in Ordinary Time

Gospel: Mark 1:21-28

In the city of Capernaum, Jesus entered the synagogue on the sabbath and began to teach. The people were spellbound by his teaching because he taught with authority and not like the scribes.

Commentary: R. Guardini

What a privilege it must have been to see the Lord at the beginning of his public ministry as he carried holiness into the crowds. How clearly he spoke to the souls of men! Pressed forward by the élan of the Spirit, he reached out to people with both hands. The Holy Spirit swept the kingdom of God forward and the human spirit was shaken to its foundations. The accounts of these first events are vibrant with spiritual power. Thus Saint Mark: *And they were astonished at his teaching, for he was teaching them as one having authority, and not as the scribes.* They were *astonished*, literally shaken out of themselves. Such was the divine power that poured from his words. Jesus' sentences were not merely correct as were those of the scribes, they were the words of one *having authority*. His speech stirred, it tore the spirit from its security, the heart from its rest; it commanded and created. It was impossible to hear and ignore.

Saint Mark's account continues with a description of the casting out of an unclean spirit. Obviously we have here a case of "possession." The Lord's acceptance of the inevitable struggle with satanic powers belongs to the kernel of his messianic consciousness. He knows that he has been sent not only to bear witness to the truth, to establish contact between God and man, but also to break the power of those forces which oppose the divine will. He is to penetrate Satan's artificial darkness with the ray of God's truth, to dispel the cramp of egoism and the brittleness of hate with God's love, to conquer evil's destructiveness with God's constructive strength. The murkiness and confusion which Satan creates in men's groping hearts are to be clarified by the holy purity of the Most High. Thus Jesus stands squarely against the powers of darkness; he strives to enter into the ensnared souls of men — to bring light to their consciences, quicken their hearts, and liberate their powers for good.

(*The Lord*, 40-41)

Romano Guardini (1885-1968), born at Verona in Italy, grew up in Mainz, and was ordained in 1910. Ten years later he was admitted to the faculty of divinity at Bonn. In 1923 he became professor of dogmatic theology at Breslau and in 1945 professor of philosophy at Tübingen. His books were widely read by the laity and had great influence especially on the younger generation. They include: *The Lord, The Faith and Modern Man, The Living God*, and *Sacred Signs*.

Fifth Sunday in Ordinary Time

Gospel: Mark 1:29-39

Upon leaving the synagogue, Jesus entered the house of Simon and Andrew with James and John. Simon's mother-in-law lay ill with a fever, and the first thing they did was to tell him about her.

Commentary: A. Hulsbosch

The many facets of our present suffering can all ultimately be reduced to the earthly experience of our relationship to God. God is invisible, while we are clothed with the dust. This means that the Godward-orientation which the Spirit has aroused in our hearts can only express itself here on earth through our contacts with other visible human beings.

If anyone who has enough to live on sees another in need and yet closes his heart against him, how can the love of God dwell in such a one? Children, we must not make love a matter of mere words or talk; it must be genuine, and show itself in our deeds. No one has ever seen God; but if we love one another, God dwells in us and his love is brought to perfection in us. Here is the proof that we dwell in him and he in us: he has given us his own Spirit.

There is always an element of suffering in the love of Christians for one another. It is measured by the extent to which we give ourselves, our person, and our possessions. There is a struggle between this act of giving and our old fallen nature. Dying to self is a full-time job where our natural tendencies are concerned.

Suffering also comes to us from the opposite side. Just as we can be a burden to others, so our fellow human beings can cause us to suffer. The classical example of such suffering in Holy Scripture is persecution for one's faith. Christians are tested by persecution. If they give way in the face of violence the test shows that they have no real love for God. On the other hand the endurance of trials, especially death for the confession of Christ, is the highest form of self-affirmation the human spirit can make and the greatest act of freedom any man or woman can attain on this earth.

Trials do not necessarily originate in ourselves or in other people. They can occur in the form of sickness or misfortunes of various kinds, and these too can demand of Christians the martyrdom of bearing witness to their faith in eternal life. Our existence on this earth is in itself a trial that requires a continual re-affirmation of faith in God; a trial that offers us the opportunity to win freedom for ourselves by overcoming. By its means we learn to rule over created things, which can now no longer harm us. They are in fact shown to be beneficial: *we know that in everything God works for good with those who love him.* Christians who are truly upheld by Christ know that nothing can any longer threaten them. *What can separate us from the love of Christ? Affliction or hardship, persecution, hunger, nakedness, peril, or the sword? It is written, "For your sake we are being put to death all day long; we are treated like sheep for slaughter." Yet in all these things we are more than conquerors through him who loved us. For I am convinced that there is nothing in death or life, in the realm of spirits or superhuman powers, in the present world or the world to come, in the forces of the universe, in heights or depths — nothing in the whole creation that can separate us from the love of God in Christ Jesus our Lord.*

Human beings can endure trials and emerge from them victorious, because Jesus has done so before them.

(*De schepping Gods,* 155-156)

Ansfried Hulsbosch, O.S.A. (1912-1973), born at Zanvoort, Holland, joined the Order of Saint Augustine in 1932. He studied philosophy and theology at Nijmegen, was ordained in 1938, and received a doctorate in theology at the Angelicum in Rome in 1941. He also obtained a doctorate in scripture at the Pontifical Biblical Institute. From 1945 to 1965 he taught New Testament exegesis at the Augustinian Seminary in Nijmegen and his Order's international college at Rome. After a long illness he died on 2 February 1973. Over the years he published many well-received articles on exegesis and theology as well as several books in the same field.

Sixth Sunday in Ordinary Time

Gospel: Mark 1:40-45

A leper approached Jesus with a request, kneeling down as he addressed him: "If you will to do so, you can cure me."

Commentary: Paul VI

Jesus' meeting with lepers is the type and the model of his meeting with every person who is restored to health and to the perfection of the original divine image and admitted again to the communion of the people of God. In these meetings Jesus showed himself as the bearer of a new life, of a fullness of humanity that had long been lost. The Mosaic laws excluded and condemned the leper, forbade anyone to approach him, speak to him, touch him. Jesus, on the contrary, proves to be, in the first place, sovereignly free with regard to the old law. He approaches, he speaks, he touches and even cures the leper; he heals him and restores his flesh to the freshness of a child's. And a leper came to him, we read in Mark, *beseeching him, and kneeling said to him, "If you will, you can make me clean."* The same thing will happen for ten other lepers. "Lepers are cleansed!": this is the sign of his Messiahship that Jesus gives to John the Baptist's disciples who had come to question him. And Jesus entrusts his own mission to his disciples: "Preach, saying, *The kingdom of heaven is at hand*...cleanse lepers." Furthermore, he solemnly affirmed that ritual purity is completely secondary, that what is really important and decisive for salvation is moral purity, that of the heart, of the will, which has nothing to do with spots on the skin or the person.

But the loving gesture of Christ, who approaches lepers comforting them and curing them, has its full and mysterious expression in the passion. Tortured and disfigured by the sweat of blood, the flagellation, the crowning with thorns, the crucifixion, the rejection by the people he had helped, he identifies himself with lepers, becomes the image and symbol of them, as the prophet

Isaiah had foreseen, contemplating the mystery of the Servant of the Lord: *He had no form or comeliness. . . . He was despised and rejected by men . . . as one from whom men hide their faces . . . we esteemed him stricken, smitten by God and afflicted.* But it is just from the wounds in Jesus' tortured body and from the power of his resurrection that life and hope gushes for all men stricken by evil and infirmity.

(*Discourses*, 29 January 1978)

Paul VI (1897-1978), born Giovanni Battista Montini, was ordained a priest in 1920 and in 1925 entered the Vatican Secretariat of State. In this service of the Church he filled several important posts until he was named archbishop of Milan by Pius XII on 1 November 1954. Montini was made a cardinal in December 1958, and elected pope on 21 June 1963. During his long pontificate he showed himself to be an intrepid pastor and a determined promoter of the decrees of the Second Vatican Council. In spite of opposition he firmly held the bark of Peter on its course into a new age.

Seventh Sunday in Ordinary Time

Gospel: Mark 2:1-12

After a lapse of several days Jesus came back to Capernaum and word got around that he was at home. At that they began to gather in great numbers. There was no longer any room for them, even around the door. While he was delivering God's word to them, some people arrived bringing a paralyzed man to him.

Commentary: C. Houselander

There is a way of contemplation through suffering. Christ taught us this way from the cross. It is a bridge of love across which God comes to the human race and the human race goes to God. To practice it is thus — you look at Christ until you become like him, just as by looking at the sun you become golden like the sun. You touch his wounds, and from them you learn the measure of his love. you share the experience of his passion with him, until through loving with his love you become one with him.

We cannot see Christ in his glory, but we can see him and touch him in human suffering. Our contemplation in the world is the contemplation of the humiliated Christ in the human race. Humanity is the veil of Veronica. It is, so to speak, the suffering face of Christ on the *via crucis*, impressed upon humanity, his face covered in blood and sweat and tears, just as we do literally see so many human faces now. This disfigurement is caused by sin; exactly as Christ's historical passion was caused by sin, so is his passion in us. It is he whom we meet every day and in every house and every street, and were it not that his love has transformed even the wounding and bruising of sin, we should meet the ugliness of despair everywhere. As it is, Christ, by giving himself to our humanity as he gave the impression of his face to the veil of Veronica, has given his own mysterious beauty and significance to every tear on the human face, to every drop of blood shed from its veins.

So it is Christ whom we look on today, in everyone, everywhere, in the hospitals, in the factories, in the streets. We see him in the wounded, in the helpless old people and the infants, in the bereaved, in the homeless, in refugees. We see him as Veronica saw him on the road to Calvary. In the helpless we see him in the swaddling bands and burial bands, in the outcasts, as he has been through all the years and is now, an outcast from his own kingdom, the human heart. Gradually, through looking at Christ in these suffering people, we begin to have some faint idea of the measure of his love.

We cannot begin to understand this without wanting to respond to such love and to comfort Christ in all people. We have got to stretch Christ in us, then, to fit the size of the cross overshadowing the whole world, just as the soldiers stretched him to fit the size of the wooden cross. The arms of Christ stretched on the cross are the widest reach there is, the only one that encircles the whole world.

(*The Comforting of Christ*, 135-138)

Caryll Houselander (1901-1954) was born at Bath and became a Catholic while still a child. After receiving a general education she went on to study art, and later used her talents in many practical ways. World War II brought out especially her literary gifts as well as her compassion as a psychiatric therapist. Her works include: *This War is the Passion* (later revised as *The Comforting of Christ*), *The Reed of God, The Dry Wood, Guilt, The Stations of the Cross,* and *The Risen Christ.*

Eighth Sunday in Ordinary Time

Gospel: Mark 2:18-22

John disciples and the Pharisees were accustomed to fast. People came to Jesus with the objection, "Why do John's disciples and those of the Pharisees fast while yours do not?" Jesus replied: "How can the guests at a wedding fast as long as the groom is still among them?"

Commentary: R. Burrows

Quite obviously Jesus enjoyed food and drink. He calmly quotes the gossip about him: *they say, "Behold, a glutton and a drunkard."* Such a censorious attitude toward his simple enjoyment must have hurt. Not only that, he realized that his attitude to the ordinary pleasures of life robbed him of spiritual authority in the eyes of the religious people of his day. John the ascetic, with his hairshirt, severe fasting and estrangement from the world, they could understand, but not this fellow who seemed to live too rooted in our workaday world. A man of God should be ascetic, not one of the ordinary folk, doing as others do. Jesus refused to change his attitude even though by so doing he might have won them. But this would have been to betray the truth and his mission. What a profound lesson lies here!

When challenged about fasting, that John's disciples fast but yours don't, he had this answer: *Can the wedding guests mourn whilst the bridegroom is with them? The days will come when the bridegroom will be taken away from them, and then they will fast.* Again the image of a wedding, the joy of marriage and its disruption when the bridegroom is taken away, proof of his simple acceptance of life as it is. What Jesus is saying here is that the fast of those who love him, who have centered their lives on him, is precisely his absence as regards the senses. This is the only fast that matters in God's eyes. Their senses must fast as that of a bride deprived of her husband. We can call it the fast of faith.

Faith is a fast, it is a refusal to put anything in the place of God, and an acceptance of the consequent sense of deprivation. Faith refuses to seek the sensible assurances our nature craves for, and insists on looking beyond, reaching out to him who cannot be savored in this life. For one who has given his heart to our Lord there is a perennial fast while this life lasts. It is in this context I think that we must look for Christian asceticism. Christian asceticism has its roots in love of Jesus, not in fear of the body and the world at large.

For the fast of faith to be real, for the Christian to maintain a hunger for God, a God who does not satisfy his senses, he must take care not so to encompass himself with the good things of this world that his need for God is not experienced. If his desire for God is genuine, and we must not confuse real desire with a feeling or emotion, then he will want to express it in concrete forms. Outward expressions strengthen the inner disposition. Hunger for God has to be worked for. It is a sustained act of choosing under the influence of grace. The lack of religious emotion, if such there be, may well form part of the fast of faith. Hunger for God is born of faith not of feeling. It is maintained by the exercise of faith. There would be something incongruous in persons insisting that they want God, yet never depriving themselves of anything, always having everything they want when they want.

Christian austerity aims at freedom and reverence; it ensures that we receive God's gift of pleasure in an ever more personal way. A Christian is dedicated to love and life; love of God and his neighbor, assuring for himself and his neighbor an increasing abundance of life. But we have a murderer in our hearts who would destroy not only ourselves but others also, and we cannot ignore him. Now although we can truly say that a Christian's aim must always be positive, yet to maintain this positive aim he must to some extent adopt a negative one.

(*To Believe in Jesus*, 70-71)

Rita Burrows, a Carmelite author, writes about Christianity in a very candid but unpopular way. She says that the way to holiness is not through dramatic renunciation, and that holiness itself is not just for the specialists: clergy and religious; holiness cannot be struggled for or won — it can only be given when asked for.

Ninth Sunday in Ordinary Time

Gospel: Mark 2:23—3:6

It happened that Jesus was walking through standing grain on the sabbath, and his disciples began to pull off heads of grain as they went along. At this the Pharisees protested: "Look! Why do they do a thing not permitted on the sabbath?"

Commentary: F. Sheen

What scandalized the Pharisees was not the breach of biblical law, but the breach of rabbinic law. Having seen what they thought was a desecration of the sabbath day, they now openly attacked our blessed Lord for something the disciples did.

The answer of our Lord was threefold: first, he appealed to the prophets, then to the law, then to one who was greater than either, namely, himself. Both instances which he quoted were those in which ceremonial niceties gave way to a higher law. Our Lord appealed to their great national hero, David, who ate the shewbread which was forbidden to all save the priests. If they allowed David to break a divine prohibition of a mere ceremonial affair in favor of bodily necessity, why should they not allow it to his disciples? When David was flying away from Saul and was hungry, our Lord said that he and his followers *went into the tabernacle, and ate the loaves set out there before God although neither he nor his followers, nor anyone else except the priests had a right to eat them.*

The Pharisees certainly would have admitted that the danger to life superseded the ceremonial law; but more than that, David was allowed to eat of this bread not just because he was hungry but because he pleaded that he was in the service of the king. The apostles, who were following our Lord, were also in the service of someone greater, and ministering to him was more important than David ministering to an earthly master.

Our Lord then answered more directly the charge of violating the Sabbath law. The ones who accused him labored in the temple on the Sabbath; they prepared sacrifices, they lit lamps; and yet because these were part of the temple service, they were not considered as violating the Sabbath law. But here, on this Sabbath, in the midst of this field of corn, and with no apparent trappings of glory stands one who is greater than the temple. *And I tell you there is one standing here who is greater than the temple.*

These profound words were blasphemy to the Pharisees, but they were another affirmation of what he said when he cleansed for the first time the temple in Jerusalem, saying that his body was a temple because the Godhead dwelt therein. In him the Godhead dwelt corporally; nowhere else on earth was God to be found except veiled in his humanity. His apostles, therefore, if they had broken a ceremonial regulation, were guiltless because they were in the service of the temple, aye, even of God himself.

(*Life of Christ*, 275-276)

Fulton J. Sheen (1895-1979), born and educated in El Paso, Illinois, USA, was ordained in 1919 and continued his philosophical and theological studies in Washington, DC, Louvain, and Rome. Appointed professor of philosophy of religion at The Catholic University of America, Washington, DC, he did not lose touch with people of simpler minds, but retained his gift as a popular preacher. He was especially well known for his radio and television talks. His numerous books include: *God and Intelligence, The Philosophy of Science, The Eternal Galilean*, and *The Mystical Body of Christ*.

Tenth Sunday in Ordinary Time

Gospel: Mark 3:20-35

Jesus came to the house with his disciples and again the crowd assembled, making it impossible for them to get any food whatsoever. When his family heard of this, they came to take charge of him, saying, "He is out of his mind."

Commentary: H. Rahner

Mary as the mother of Christ is also the mother who not only gave birth to our new life, but who protects our continued life of virtue, and who daily announces the Church's power as a mother over the growth of our spiritual lives.

The fathers of the early Church had a special fondness for connecting this aspect of the mystery of Mary and the Church, as concerning our own growth in holiness, with a particular event in the gospel. It is a reply of our Lord regarding his mother, which has perhaps seemed to us as strange as his reply at Cana. We all know the passage: *And one said to him: Behold, your mother and your brethren stand without, seeking you. But he answering him that told him, said: Who is my mother, and who are my brethren? And stretching forth his hand toward his disciples, he said: Behold my mother and my brethren. For whosoever shall do the will of my Father that is in heaven, he is my brother, and sister, and mother.*

These words, which at first sight seem to be a denial of his human and earthly relationship with his mother, are in fact the highest praise he could give his mother: for who of all mankind had so perfectly fulfilled the will of the heavenly Father as the Virgin had done, when in virtue of her *fiat mihi* she had become the mother of the eternal son? Furthermore, his answer implies that from now on in the kingdom of heaven it is his mother's *fiat* that will find an echo in the hearts of all who do the will of the

Father in following him. And it is precisely of these his followers that Christ says that they are in a mystical sense his mother.

If therefore the Church is mystically the company of those who do the will of the Father, she is indeed Mary in the world, the mother of Christ who gives birth every day. She is indeed all that our spiritual life stands for, since this is nothing more nor less than the daily fulfillment of the will of the Father. Here is a new motherly relationship to Christ, whose desire is daily to be born in our hearts, and in us, and through us to grow to his perfect manhood, to the mature measure of his fullness.

This in early times was the thought of the great Origen on the spiritual life: for him the Christian's life after baptism is seen as the growth of Christ himself within the motherly hearts of the faithful: "Just as an infant is formed in the womb, so it seems to me that the Word of God is in the heart of a soul, which has received the grace of baptism and then forms within itself the word of faith ever more glorious and more plain."

(Our Lady and the Church, 70-72)

Hugo Rahner, S.J. (1900-1968), older and not as well known as his world-famous brother, was nonetheless a highly regarded theologian and historian in his own right. Born at Pfullendorf, Germany, he joined the Society of Jesus in 1919. After his ordination, he became a professor at Innsbruck University, and from 1949-1956 he was rector of the prestigious International College, the Canisianum at Innsbruck. Before his death he published books on a variety of subjects, including *St. Ignatius of Loyola, Our Lady and the Church, Greek Myths and Christian Mysteries,* and *A Theology of Proclamation.*

Eleventh Sunday in Ordinary Time

Gospel: Mark 4:26-34

Jesus said to the crowd: "This is how it is with the reign of God. A man scatters seed on the ground. He goes to bed and gets up day after day. Through it all the seed sprouts and grows without his knowing how it happens."

Commentary: R. Benson

Here is Christ himself saying, as plainly as words can do it, that the kingdom of heaven will utterly change its appearance from being like a small, round seed, simple in shape and color and texture, to the semblance of a vast, elaborate, glorious tree, of a thousand surfaces and curves, of innumerable branches, twigs, leaves, fibers, and roots; from a seed which a bird can eat, to a tree in which a colony of birds may live.

Here is Saint Paul, whom I now remember saying again and again that the Church is the *body of Christ*, declaring that body in his days to be as the body of a child, containing indeed the structure of an athlete, his limbs, his possibilities, but not actually expressing them; and that this body will be gradually *edified* in the *unity* — not *diversity* — of *the faith, and of the knowledge of the Son of God*, until it is full-grown — until it gradually corresponds in fact in its outward appearance and stature with the mind and spirit of Christ, which have been in it from the beginning!

For I am more than the oak and the mustard-tree: I am the very vine of God, *brought out of Egypt long ago*. My seed fell in a ball of fire with the sound of wind; and from that moment I have lived indeed. I thrust my white shoots in the darkness of the catacombs, and forced my way through the cracks of Caesar's falling palaces; my early grapes were trodden under foot, crushed in the winepress of rack and prison; I am blown upon by every wind that blows, by calumny and criticism from the north, by passion and fury in the south and west. I am pruned year by year with sharp knives forged in death and hell, yet grasped by the hand of the Father who is my husbandman. And yet I live, and shall live, till my Beloved comes down to taste the fruits of the garden.

For I am planted by the river of salvation, watered by the tears and blood of saints, breathed upon by the spirit of God who alone can make the spices to flow forth. More than that, I am mystically one with my Beloved already; it is his heart's blood that flows in my veins; his strength that sustains me; for he is the vine, my boughs are his branches; and I am nothing save in him and them. It is for this cause then that I spring up indomitable; that I stretch my boughs to the river, and my branches to the sea, that my shadow is in all lands; that the wild birds lodge in my branches, the dove and the eagle together; that the fierce beasts crouch beside my roots, *the wolf beside the lamb, and the leopard by the kid*. It is for this that I am older than the centuries, younger than yesterday, eternal, undying and divine.

(*The Religion of the Plain Man*, 76-77.87-89)

Robert Hugh Benson (1871-1914), son of Edward White Benson, archbishop of Canterbury, was ordained an Anglican priest in 1894, entered an Anglican religious community in 1898, became a Roman Catholic in 1903, and was ordained a Catholic priest in 1904. He published sermons and popular novels on religious themes.

Twelfth Sunday in Ordinary Time

Gospel: Mark 4:35-41

One day as evening drew on Jesus said to his disciples: "Let us cross over to the farther shore." It happened that a bad squall blew up.

Commentary: J. Hoffmeister

The words uttered by the holy mother of Samuel are forever true: *The Lord kills and makes alive; he brings down to the nether world and brings back.* What does it mean, then, that such a great storm arose while the Lord our Savior was with his disciples in the boat? We should certainly not think that this happened without reason or by chance. Listen then to what I am about to say, and reflect carefully on it. This storm seems to prefigure what the Apostle says elsewhere: *All who would live a godly life in Christ Jesus will suffer persecution.* The disciples had frequently crossed the lake without Christ and also without any danger, but now, when they are carrying Christ with them, they encounter such storm winds that they lose heart and despair of their lives.

So too it often happens that people in this world who do not yet believe in Christ and follow the divine call live very happy lives without any external danger to their possessions, but when they take Christ into their boats, that is, when they begin to believe in Christ and follow the divine call, they soon run into all kinds of afflictions. The wise man is therefore correct in warning each of us: *Son, when you enter the service of God, prepare your soul for trials.*

This is not to be understood as meaning that many storms and many tribulations are a lasting and sure sign of godliness, for the wicked too at times have their afflictions and scourges. Let me put it briefly: the Lord sometimes scourges his own in this life in order to test them and hold them to their duty and to keep it from appearing that they serve him for the sake of temporal happiness. According to Satan, it was for the sake of such happiness that patient Job served God. Furthermore, the Lord at times scourges the wicked so that they may change their ways or, if they refuse to change, they may suffer lasting punishment here and in the world to come. For if the Lord were constantly to shower blessings on the good and misfortunes on the wicked, there would seem to be no room for a judgment after this life. If he were constantly to scourge the devout, many would think he hated their devotion. But enough of this.

Let me add this point: after my sermon is finished, we must cross the sea of this world with Christ. What then is to be said of the fact that during this great storm Christ sleeps? He certainly did not simply pretend to be asleep; he really slept a natural sleep. For just as he felt hunger and thirst, as other human beings did, and was weary, and wept, and experienced all the other human weaknesses (except for sin), so too like other human beings he grew sleepy and slept as nature required. At the same time, however, the fact that the Lord slept and that while he slept the great storm arose is not without its hidden meaning. For from this incident we see and learn that all our human affairs tend to ruin if the Lord does not take them into his hands. With good reason he says elsewhere: *Without me you can do nothing.* At times he allows us to act as we wish, in order that when we realize that we are getting nowhere, we may immediately turn back to him.

What, then, are we to do when this kind of storm arises? We are to do what the apostles did, as described by one of their number, Matthew: *And they came to him and awakened him, saying: "Lord, save us, we are perishing."* Let us do the same: let us go to him not on bodily feet but with the heart's affections.

(Sermons, Fourth Sunday after Epiphany, fol. XXXIII-XXXIV)

Johannes Hoffmeister, O.S.A. (-1547) was numbered among the best defenders of the Catholic cause in southern Germany, especially by his numerous writings in defense of the faith. In 1545 he preached at the Diet of Worms. The needs of Germany kept Hoffmeister from attending the Council of Trent. He died at Günzburg, Germany, on 21 August 1547.

Thirteenth Sunday in Ordinary Time

Gospel: Mark 5:21-43

When Jesus had crossed back to the other side of the Sea of Galilee in the boat, a large crowd gathered around him and he stayed close to the lake. One of the officials of the synagogue, a man named Jairus, came near. Seeing Jesus, he fell at his feet and made this earnest appeal: "My little daughter is critically ill."

Commentary: C. Stuhlmueller

*T*he passage from the opening chapters of the Book of Wisdom states clearly: God does not rejoice in the destruction of the living. The gospel exemplifies this fact in the tender and determined way that Jesus restores life and health under seemingly impossible circumstances.

In the gospel we find that Jesus also claimed these people as his own. He sought out the sick "little daughter" of the synagogue official. He was also "conscious that healing power had gone out from him" when the woman with a long-term hemorrhage had touched him. In each of these miracles Jesus overcame traditional custom and taboos in a way that a modern reader may miss. In the case of the woman, she touched the hem of his cloak; in the other instance, we read that Jesus took the little girl by the hand. Twice Jesus became ceremonially unclean and was not permitted to enter the synagogue or temple to pray liturgically or publicly. It was not that Jesus intended to fly in the face of tradition. Rather, he acted spontaneously, lovingly but also in a way that he was willing to defend.

When Jesus turned around in the crowd and asked, "Who touched me?" the woman was rightly fearful. She began to tremble, in fact. She had made this holy man unclean! Jesus drew public attention to the fact, however, not in any way to reprimand her but rather to praise her faith. This faith, he assured her, has cured you.

Struggling with illness and seeking health were good actions. It was all the better to include the Lord in this search and to believe in the power of miracles. Jesus, in raising the little girl back to life, at once became conscious of her human needs. "He told them to give her something to eat!"

Once the miracle has taken place, Jesus wanted the people to settle down again in their ordinary family life. "Give her something to eat!" Jesus was blessing our human existence; he was making it possible for us to enjoy physically the normal joys of life. We recall the words of the Book of Wisdom: The creatures of the world are wholesome.

To enjoy we must share. A selfish person is never a happy person. Neither is a selfish person "wholesome," in the literal meaning of the word. Such a one lacks the quality of being "whole," that is, of belonging to the whole family of God's people.

(*Biblical Meditations for Ordinary Time*, 294-296)

Carroll Stuhlmueller, C.P. (1923-1994), member of the Congregation of the Passion since 1943, was professor of Old Testament studies at The Catholic Theological Union in Chicago and the only male member of the steering committee of the Women's Ordination Conference. A past president of the Catholic Biblical Association, he served as general editor of *The Bible Today*, as editor of *Old Testament Message*, a twenty-three-volume international commentary series, and on the editorial boards of the *Journal of Biblical Literature* and the *Catholic Biblical Quarterly*. He was the author of twenty-three books and many scholarly and popular articles on the Bible.

Fourteenth Sunday in Ordinary Time

Gospel: Mark 6:1-6

Jesus went to his own part of the country followed by his disciples. When the sabbath came he began to teach in the synagogue in a way that kept his large audience amazed. They said: "Where did he get all this? What kind of wisdom is he endowed with? How is it that such miraculous deeds are accomplished by his hands?"

Commentary: L. Boros

The people of Nazareth thought from what he has carried out elsewhere, as in Capernaum, that he is a great miracle worker. Now he should relieve our suffering. This is his home; he knows many of us and grew up with us. Our fate should move him most deeply. He has already shown us that he is merciful. Why, then, does he show no mercy to us? The people of Nazareth possibly imagined that their village would now be transformed into a paradise. Sorrow, distress, and suffering would be taken away from them in one blow. Jesus perceived their thoughts. *And he said to them, "Doubtless you will quote to me this proverb, 'Physician, heal yourself; what we have heard you did at Capernaum, do here also in your own country.' "* Jesus' answer was a decisive negative. He based his attitude on two examples from the Old Testament. The point of his justification is that miracles are not for men. The miraculous action must take place where God "sends" the prophet. *When they heard this, all in the synagogue were filled with wrath. And they rose up and put him out of the city, and led him to the brow of the hill on which their city was built, that they might throw him down headlong. But passing through the midst of them he went away.*

The anger of the people of Nazareth is the expression of human confusion when faced with this man Jesus. Anyone who regards him as merely a man will meet with the same temptation. Here is a man who possesses superhuman powers and in spite of this will

100

not help the helpless, although he has already shown that he is merciful. Any reference to the will of God sounds like a lame excuse in this case. Only one explanation is left, but it is one which the people of Nazareth did not find possible: that of faith, and, moreover, of faith in his divinity. For if, in fact, he is both God and man, then a possible way of understanding him is revealed. The God-Man is our Redeemer. But as our Redeemer his task was not to take our suffering away, however much he may have wished to do so, but to share in our suffering himself, to sanctify it, and to make it a means of redemption for each of us. Redemption does not mean magic, but the opening up of a new possibility at the point where what is human has come to an end, the opening up of a new dimension and not the removal of reality. What is human must persist with all its darkness. But into this darkness there comes the call of redemption, a call to live out our wretched existence in a new way, on the basis of new principles and promises. This is redemption. Anything else would be magic. But let no one deceive himself: to endure this was a heart-breaking act even for one who was God and man. What an immense tension he had to endure! On the one hand, his mercy urged him irresistibly to give his help, while at the same time his hands were bound by the very nature of his divine task. His soul was martyred throughout his life. At this point an abyss opens before us, and the longer we gaze into it, the more we are seized by a holy trembling at the sight of Jesus.

(*God Is With Us*, 64-66)

Ladislas Boros (1917-), born in Budapest, was ordained in 1957. He attended Jesuit houses of study in Hungary, Austria, Italy, and France, and also the University of Munich, where he received his doctorate in philosophy. He was dean of studies of philosophy and religion in the theological faculty of the University of Innsbruck. He gained international fame with his work in the area of the theology of death. Among his works are: *The Moment of Truth, Pain and Providence, Meeting God in Man*, and *God Is With Us*.

Fifteenth Sunday in Ordinary Time

Gospel: Mark 6:7-13

Jesus summoned the Twelve and began to send them out two by two, giving them authority over unclean spirits.

Commentary: Paul VI

The Church owes its origin to the preaching of the gospel by Jesus and the Twelve. Its foundation was both the aim and as it were the connatural fruit of their labors; more than anything else it was the immediate and self-evident result of the command to go out and teach all nations. *Those who accepted Peter's word were baptized. That very day about three thousand souls joined the community. Daily the Lord added to their number those destined to be saved.*

Once born of this apostolic mission, the Church is in turn commissioned by Jesus to go forth and preach. Now that he has returned to his Father in glory, the Church remains in the world as an obscure yet luminous sign of his new mode of presence, reminding us that though the Lord has gone away he is still in our midst. The Church is a continuation and extension of his presence, called above all to carry on the mission of Jesus and his work of evangelization without ceasing. Never can the Christian community be shut in on itself. Nourished by fervent prayer, the hearing of the word and the teaching of the apostles, the exercise of brotherly love and the breaking of bread, its inner life cannot attain its full vigor unless it becomes a witness, gaining favor with the people and converting souls by preaching and proclaiming the Good News. This mission of evangelization is laid upon the entire Church, and the efforts of each individual member are important for the whole.

However, as the herald of the gospel the Church begins its task by evangelizing itself. Since it is a fellowship of believers, a fellowship of living and shared hope and a fellowship of fraternal love, the Church needs continually to hear the tenets of its faith, the grounds for its hope and the new commandment of love. As the People of God living in the world and frequently tempted by false gods, the Church experiences the constant need to be reminded of those mighty deeds of God which brought about its conversion, to hear the Lord's call anew, and to be gathered together once more into unity. In short, the Church always needs to listen to the gospel message, because only by so doing can it maintain its vigor and zeal and the power to proclaim that message to others. The only effective way for the Church to evangelize the world is to evangelize itself and to be continually converted and renewed.

The Church is the depositary of the Good News which has to be made known to the whole human race. The promises of the New Covenant already realized in Jesus Christ, the teaching of our Lord and the apostles, the word of life, the well-springs of God's grace and loving kindness and the way of salvation — all these have been entrusted to the Church which treasures them as a life-giving and precious heritage. They are the substance of the gospel and consequently of evangelization, a talent not to be hidden away in a napkin but to be displayed before the eyes of all.

Having itself been evangelized and sent out to preach, the Church in its turn sends out evangelists. It puts the word of salvation into their mouths, expounds to them the message entrusted to its own safe keeping, hands on to them its own mandate, and so sends them out to preach. It is not themselves or their personal theories that they are commissioned to disseminate, but the gospel of which neither they nor the Church have been appointed absolute masters with full authority to exercise their own judgment. They are rather to regard themselves as stewards whose duty it is to pass on the Good News with complete fidelity.

(Evangelii nuntiandi, 15)

Paul VI (1897-1978), born Giovanni Battista Montini, was ordained a priest in 1920 and in 1925 entered the Vatican Secretariat of State. In this service of the Church he filled several important posts until he was named archbishop of Milan by Pius XII on 1 November 1954. Montini was made a cardinal in December 1958, and elected pope on 21 June 1963. During his long pontificate he showed himself to be an intrepid pastor and a determined promoter of the decrees of the Second Vatican Council. In spite of opposition he firmly held the bark of Peter on its course into a new age.

Sixteenth Sunday in Ordinary Time

Gospel: Mark 6:30-34

The apostles returned to Jesus and reported to him all that they had done and what they had taught. Jesus said to them: "Come by yourselves to an out-of-the-way place and rest a little."

Commentary: L. Suenens

Modern life is lived at high tension; nerves get frayed, the pace of life is intense. Whatever it costs, we must learn how to stop, when we need to, and draw a quiet breath. Men and women solve the problem of necessary recreation by taking more weekends and holidays. That is a step forward. But we must still learn how to relax, how to avoid being unbalanced by amusements, how to measure out this rhythm of fatigue and repose, work and recreation, in the required mixture. It is most important that rest should be soothing and that recreation, as the word implies, should re-create, create us over again, give us new life, a fresh start. We are a long way from that: how many tourists do their touring on the piece-work system! They eat up the miles, they tear through the countryside, see nothing, and come back more exhausted than when they started. This applies not only to tourism, but to the cinema and TV, and it can even be true of reading if we fail to learn the art of relaxing in order to work better.

In order to acquire this art, we must learn particularly how to take advantage of the little opportunities life has to offer and become children at heart again. We must not live at such an intensive, hustling pace that we no longer have time to...have time. To be relaxed makes one accessible to others.

We must learn, or re-learn, to have time. Our Lord himself did not want his apostles to live in a state of perpetual tension. He urged them to *come away into a quiet place*: *rest a little*, he said to them, the best of himself and his message. Our Lord paid a great deal of attention to time and the gradual approach. How often he said to his apostles: *It is not for you to know, now, what I am doing; but you will understand it afterward*, or *My time has not yet come; the time is coming.*

We stand in need of rest; rest in the ordinary sense of the word, and also rest in God. We must find a place for him in the bustle of the day; a place for private prayer, for slow and meditative reading. We need this "oxygen." No luxury this; it is one of our vital necessities. It is a good thing to sit down, like Mary, at the feet of the Master before we go on to carry out our indispensable daily tasks. In the midst of work, we must keep our hearts open to God. It helps so much to keep things in their proper proportion if we keep a window open to heaven.

(Christian Life Day by Day, 94-98)

Leon Joseph Suenens (1904-1996) was born in Brussels, Belgium, and after having entered the seminary he studied at the Gregorian University in Rome and earned a doctorate in theology in 1927. After ordination as a priest in 1927 he taught at the seminary from 1930-1940. From 1940-1945 he taught philosophy at the seminary in Malines, Belgium, and was auxiliary bishop (1945-1961) and the archbishop of Malines from 1961. He was very prominent at the Second Vatican Council and in the post-conciliar era of Vatican II.

Seventeenth Sunday in Ordinary Time

Gospel: John 6:1-15

Jesus crossed the sea of Galilee to the shore of Tiberias; a vast crowd kept following him because they saw the signs he was performing for the sick. Jesus then went up the mountain and sat down there with his disciples.

Commentary: J. Hoffmeister

The Lord *gives food to all flesh*, but in doing so he uses his creatures as his ministers: sun and moon, snow and rain, soil, and the plowing, sowing, reaping, and so on of human beings; and he follows the same pattern in the spiritual realm. *I have planted*, says Paul, *Apollo watered, but God gave the increase*. As Son of Man the Lord Jesus received the heavenly bread of true doctrine from his Father; the apostles received it from Christ, and others from the apostles, and thus successively fed the entire Church on the one heavenly bread. For the teaching of the true and Catholic Church is one and the same; it can be explained more clearly, but it cannot and must not be altered or changed. For as Paul testifies, there is *one God, one faith, and one baptism*.

John the evangelist tells us that Jesus gave thanks to the Father. What need does Christ have of such ceremonies? Is he not the Word of God and very God? He spoke and things were made; he commanded and they were created. Why, then, does he not now simply command that the loaves be multiplied? Christ could indeed have multiplied the loaves without uttering even a single word and simply willing it, but he thought it good to make use of these ceremonies in order, first of all, to let the crowd know that he is not teaching some other God beside the true creator of heaven and earth and that he performs his miracles not by trickery but by the power of God in heaven.

Secondly, he also wanted to teach what thanksgiving is and what power it possesses. For by this thanksgiving the five loaves and two fish are blessed, increased, and multiplied to such an extent that not only are five thousand men, to say nothing of the women and children, fed generously, but twelve baskets of fragments are collected as well. I shall add this further point: Christ gives thanks to God the Father and thus multiplies a few loaves, in order to teach us that we do not usually experience multiplication in our affairs unless we have first thanked God for few or little things and have used them with gratitude.

We must reflect carefully on all these points in order to learn the correct and upright way of multiplying riches or other blessings of God. For the corruption of their nature leads human beings to think that no matter what blessings they receive from God, they have received less than they deserve. Therefore they bend all their effort and planning to increase what they have received and possess; if they cannot do it uprightly and justly, then they will do it by wicked and unjust means, and in any way they can, provided only they do increase it.

(Sermons, Laetare Sunday, fol. LXXVII)

Johannes Hoffmeister, O.S.A. (-1547) was numbered among the best defenders of the Catholic cause in southern Germany, especially by his numerous writings in defense of the faith. In 1545 he preached at the Diet of Worms. The needs of Germany kept Hoffmeister from attending the Council of Trent. He died at Günzburg, Germany, on 21 August 1547.

Eighteenth Sunday
in Ordinary Time

Gospel: John 6:24-35

When the crowd saw that neither Jesus nor his disciples were at the place where Jesus had eaten the bread, they too embarked in the boats and went to Capernaum looking for Jesus.

Commentary: A. de Orozco

Is not the life more than the food, and the body more than the garment? This is a most effective argument for those who are not stupid. It is an argument from the greater to the lesser. How can someone who has given you more important things refuse you lesser things? My friend, the good God has given you life, which is more valuable than any food; far be it from him, then, to refuse you the food which sustains life. Furthermore, as Job says, he has with his own hands formed and given you a body that is more valuable than any gold-embroidered garment; therefore he will also in his kindness give you the lesser gift, namely, the clothing that covers the body.

He warns us against allowing concern for temporal blessings received to cause us distress. Would that we were constantly mindful in our hearts of the still greater blessings which this most generous of Fathers bestows upon us, lest being forgetful of them we be more anxious than we should about temporal goods which are so unimportant. How foolish they are who do not entrust themselves to God with full confidence in this kindest of Fathers! The ignorant crowd makes its wretched state twice as bad by toiling both in body and in spirit. They sow and then are fearful and anxious lest a thief steal the grain or fire consume it. How empty the things human beings worry about! If we are to dispel vain anxiety, we need to think often of the blessings God bestows on us; otherwise worry and anxiety will greatly torment us. Happy they who everywhere sing with the royal prophet. *What return shall I make to the Lord for all that he has given to me?* (Ps 115:12).

Let me go a step further, brothers. Not only has God in his goodness given us life and a body without any worry on our part — this God who, as the Apostle testifies, gives more abundantly than we ask or can understand. In addition, our Savior has given himself to us as food, so that daily we eat his holy body and drink his blessed red blood. Behold a pledge than which there can be no greater! and it is given so that we his children may have unlimited hope in him and may not perish through lack of trust in him. Why should we exhaust ourselves for corruptible food when we are fed at the sacred altar of the nectar-sweet food of the angels? But the mind that is doubtful and full of worry about divine providence feels less at ease because it has little faith.

(Third Sunday After Epiphany, Sermon 10, *Opera Omnia* I, 138-139)

Alonso de Orozco, O.S.A. (1500-1591) studied at the University of Salamanca before entering the Augustinian novitiate there. His main apostolates in the Order were preaching and writing, and although he was chosen as royal preacher at the Spanish court, he preferred to speak to poor and simple people. His religious life was marked by a spirit of fraternity, gospel simplicity, and moderation in speech. As an ascetic and great mystic, he suffered crisis and spiritual aridity from 1522 to 1551. He was beatified by Pope Leo XIII in 1882.

Nineteenth Sunday in Ordinary Time

Gospel: John 6:41-51

The Jews started to murmur in protest because Jesus claimed: "I am the bread that came down from heaven." They kept saying: "Is this not Jesus, the son of Joseph?"

Commentary: G. Preston

Christ offers himself in the eucharist as food and drink. In eating and drinking at the eucharistic table we are indicating our readiness to eat and drink, to feed on him, in the multiple ways in which he offers himself as our food and drink. The author of *The Imitation of Christ* talks about the table of the word as well as of the sacrament. Ignatius of Antioch tells us that faith is the flesh, the substance of the Christian life. "Believe and you have fed," says Augustine. Basil remarks that the Christian eats and drinks the blood of the Word when he shares in his coming and in his teaching. But however we eat the flesh of the Son of man and drink his blood, whether sacramentally in the eucharist, or at the table of his word, or by care for his suffering members, it is always the case that it cannot be done once and for all. We have to go on doing it. The eucharist is the bread and the wine which of itself creates hunger and thirst, the nourishment which feeds desire and longing, longing for the coming of the kingdom of God.

What we are doing in the eucharist is profoundly involved with that coming. Whenever we eat this bread and drink this cup we placard the death of the Lord *until he comes*. Until he comes we are trying out for size what it will be like when he comes. He is food for the journey and the end of the journey is not yet. We pray for him to come, and still he comes only in signs, though the signs are his real presence. He comes only in signs, and so in the presence of those signs transformed into him, we tell God that we are still waiting in hope for the coming of our Savior Jesus Christ. Just at the moment when we are more than ever conscious that he is with us, we say such things as "Christ will come again" or "Lord Jesus, come in glory," or we say that we are doing this until he comes in glory. Yet we pretend that the end really is now: we eat together at the banquet God has prepared for us, and drink from the overflowing cup he has mingled and poured out for us. Again and again we wish peace to one another, that peace and unity which belong to the kingdom where the Lord Jesus lives forever and ever. It is a prophetic sign, pretending for awhile that he has come, roughing out his coming here and now.

We come thereby into a situation where what unites us is the word of God and one loaf and a common cup; this loaf and cup derive their significance from their relation to the death of Jesus to this world and his living to God. In fact they simply are this Jesus dead to sin and alive to God, the one who is God's way of being man. This loaf and cup, which are the way that new and only true humanity is embodied in our world, are what make us a unity. They are what make us the body of Christ here and now, even as in the kingdom the unity of all mankind will be Christ, the Lamb of the Apocalypse with the marks of slaughter still upon him, the hanged man with the wounds that never healed but were glorified. Here and now we let ourselves be taken into that and live as though that were already so, just as in the liberated zones of occupied territories people now and again live for awhile as though the liberation were final. By doing this we are set toward our destiny more fervently. We already feel ourselves at home in what is yet to be and more displaced in what still is. Here and now, with these very unrisen people with all their quirks and foibles and sins, many of them well known enough to me, I pretend that the end of all things which is the meaning of all things has come already. The eucharist is the sacrament of peace and unity between us.

(God's Way to Be Human, 87-89)

Geoffrey Preston, O.P. was born in Cheshire, England, the son of the local blacksmith. He was educated at the nearby grammar school and Durham University; it was during this time that he moved from Methodism through Anglicanism to the Catholic Church. A man of wide intellectual culture, he still retained his peasant simplicity and the habit of deep pondering on the word of God which he had learned as a Methodist. Entering the Dominican Order, he was made novice master after nine years. He died at the early age of forty-one.

Twentieth Sunday in Ordinary Time

Gospel: John 6:51-58

Jesus said to the crowds: "I myself am the living bread come down from heaven. If anyone eats this bread he shall live forever; the bread I will give is my flesh, for the life of the world."

Commentary: Elizabeth of the Trinity

*H*e who eats my flesh and drinks my blood, remains in me and I in him. The first sign of love is this: that Jesus has given us his flesh to eat and his blood to drink. The property of love is to be always giving and always receiving. Now the love of Christ is generous. All that he has, all that he is, he gives; all that we have, all that we are, he takes away. He asks for more than we of ourselves are capable of giving. He has an immense hunger which wants to devour us absolutely. He enters even into the marrow of our bones, and the more lovingly we allow him to do so, the more fully we savor him. He knows that we are poor, but he pays no heed to it and does not spare us. He himself becomes in us his own bread, first burning up, in his love, all our vices, faults, and sins. Then when he sees that we are pure, he comes like a gaping vulture that is going to devour everything. He wants to consume our life in order to change it into his own; ours, full of vices, his, full of grace and glory and all prepared for us, if only we will renounce ourselves.

Even if our eyes were good enough to see this avid appetite of Christ who hungers for our salvation, all our efforts would not prevent us from disappearing into his open mouth. Now this sounds absurd, but those who love will understand! When we receive Christ with interior devotion, his blood, full of warmth and glory, flows into our veins and a fire is enkindled in our depths. We receive the likeness of his virtues, and he lives in us and we in him. He gives us his soul with the fullness of grace, by which the soul perseveres in love and praise of the Father! Love draws its object into itself; we draw Jesus into ourselves; Jesus draws us into himself. Then carried above ourselves into love's interior, seeking God, we go to meet him, to meet his Spirit, which is his love, and this love burns us, consumes us, and draws us into unity where beatitude awaits us. Jesus meant this when he said: *With great desire have I desired to eat this pasch with you.*

(*The Complete Works*, volume 1, 100-101)

Elizabeth of the Trinity (1880-1906), a Carmelite nun born Elizabeth Catez near Bourges, France, was influenced by John of the Cross, Thérèse of Lisieux, and Jan van Ruysbroeck. Her spirituality, which leads through deepening silence to the indwelling Trinity, is strongly Christocentric. She sees transformation into the image of God taking place on earth as individuals relive the mysteries of the Incarnate Word in their personal humanity. In the Letter of Paul to the Ephesians, she found her "new name," Praise of Glory (1:12). Her writings emphasize heaven and eternity permeating every temporal moment. She died in 1906 of Addison's disease.

Twenty-First Sunday in Ordinary Time

Gospel: John 6:60-69

Many of the disciples of Jesus remarked: "This sort of talk is hard to endure! How can anyone take it seriously?"

Commentary: J. Hoffmeister

There are some of you who do not believe.

What do they not believe? They do not believe that Christ is the Son of God and has come down from heaven into this world. They do not believe that Christ is both spirit and flesh, that is, true God and true human being. They do not believe that the words of Christ Jesus our Savior are spirit and life, that is, they do not believe that Christ can do everything by his word alone. These persons are poles apart from the man who said: Only say the word, and my servant shall be healed.

Since they did not believe all these truths, it is not surprising that they did not believe Christ's flesh can be given to us as food. Note, therefore, that Christ does not say to the Jews: "You do not understand"; no, he says: *You do not believe*, for faith is needed here, and a shift from things visible to things invisible. Note, too, that when Christ reveals the hidden thoughts of their hearts, he very clearly shows that he is God, who alone is called "searcher of hearts." For the Lord knew not only who they were who already believed in him, but also the one who was to betray him.

After this, many of his disciples turned back and no longer walked with him.

The foolish find wise sayings hard to accept. For just as sunlight seems a hindrance to weak eyes and dark places better for them, so sick souls feel an aversion for a more perfect discipline and reject discourse that is filled with good thoughts, while they embrace useless frivolities as most pleasurable. That is just how the Jews act in the present situation; when they fail to understand what Christ says, they do not ask the Lord for a fuller explanation but

114

go off contemptuous of him and thinking to themselves that he has been talking like a drunkard. Why did they act in this way? Because they took offense at the lowliness of the Christ whom they saw ever before them, and did not weigh his words and deeds, which they were constantly hearing and seeing.

But what of Christ's apostles? Did they too go away? By no means! In fact Christ asks them whether they too will leave him, but *Simon Peter answered him: "Lord, to whom shall we go? You have the words of eternal life, and we believe and have come to know that you are the Christ, the Son of God."*

Everything now becomes clear. You see the reason why those others went away but the apostles remained. Those who went away judged Christ to be a carpenter's son. Those who remained believed him to be the Son of God and one who could certainly give believers everlasting life. Let us too, therefore, believe whatever promises the Lord Jesus Christ makes to us; let us accept what he gives us, hope for what is in store for us, and fulfill what he commands. In this way, refreshed by his body and blood, we will live for ever with him. May this be our lot by the grace of our Lord Jesus Christ, who is blessed for endless ages. Amen.

(Sermons, Post iudica, fol. XCII)

Johannes Hoffmeister, O.S.A. (-1547) was numbered among the best defenders of the Catholic cause in southern Germany, especially by his numerous writings in defense of the faith. In 1545 he preached at the Diet of Worms. The needs of Germany kept Hoffmeister from attending the Council of Trent. He died at Günzburg, Germany, on 21 August 1547.

Twenty-Second Sunday in Ordinary Time

Gospel: Mark 7:1-8.14-15.21-23   The Pharisees and some of the experts in the law who had come from Jerusalem gathered around Jesus. They had observed a few of his disciples eating meals without having purified — that is to say, washing — their hands.

Commentary: R. Knox

If our Lord seems to impair the effectiveness of his mission by keeping too quiet about it, or by delivering his message in terms which people can't understand, we must suppose that he had some good reason for doing so. But what is even more difficult to account for, is what you may call his deliberate disregard of appearances. He is always shocking his fellow countrymen by doing the wrong things, the things they have been taught not to do. Here is this ancient people of the Jews, whose whole notion of religion is bound up with the law of Moses. It has been their ideal of life for centuries; they have gone through unheard-of persecutions rather than be false to it. Oh, no doubt the provisions of the law have grown more complicated and more exacting as time went on; that is the nature of law everywhere. No doubt, through poring over it and brooding over it for so long, its most fanatical supporters, the Pharisees, have developed an outlook of legalism. But it is the best light they have, and they are, on the whole, the most conscientious part of the nation. Now, why is it that our Lord is always going out of his way, or so it seems, to flout their favorite scruples? Always telling people to carry their beds on the sabbath day; sitting down to eat without the ceremonial washing of hands that had become customary; surrounding himself with publicans and sinners, with people who had almost lost their consciousness of Jewish nationality, who imitated the Gentiles' ways and did the Gentiles' work for them? Why did our Lord want to come to earth as a Jew, and then throw overboard all these cherished observances of Judaism?

It was, surely, because he saw one failing, among several others, as characteristic of the Jewish nation in his day. They had too much regard for appearances; they were always bothering about what other people would say. And he saw that this failing was not confined to the Jewish nation; it is common to the human race as a whole, and it is uncommonly common to you and me. Against that background of shams and pietisms, the straightforwardness of his nature revolted. It was one of the lessons he came to teach us, that this craving for the good opinion of others is a disastrous thing. Against the people who were ready to clean the outside of cup and dish, the part that showed, leaving the inside to go dirty, against the people who made long prayers and swallowed up the property of widows while they were doing it, he fulminated in accents of satire that have passed into the vocabulary of the human race. And he would be contemptuous of appearances, in protest against the spirit which thinks of appearances and nothing else.

We are as God sees us. That is what is really wrong about human respect; it's the habit of asking "What will people say?" If we cultivate it, if we live for human applause, we fall under the condemnation of those Pharisees who "valued their credit with men higher than their credit with God."

(*A Retreat for Lay People*, 105-109)

Ronald Knox (1881-1951), son of E. A. Knox, one-time bishop of Manchester, England, was educated at Eton and Oxford. Already noted for the brilliance of his mind, he was appointed chaplain of Trinity College, Oxford, and became a leading figure among Anglo-Catholics. In 1917 he was received into the Roman Catholic Church and ordained two years later. He taught for a time at Saint Edmund's Ware and was chaplain to the Catholic undergraduates at Oxford from 1936-1939. At the request of the hierarchy he then devoted himself to making a new English translation of the entire bible. The New Testament was first published in 1945 and the Old in 1949. As a writer on a wide range of subjects, Knox's thought is often strikingly original and his style characterized by wit.

Twenty-Third Sunday in Ordinary Time

Gospel: Mark 7:31-37

Jesus left Tyrian territory and returned by way of Sidon to the sea of Galilee, into the district of the Ten Cities. Some people brought him a deaf man who had a speech impediment and begged him to lay his hand on him.

Commentary: P. Parsch

*L*et us consider the account given in today's gospel. Christ is in Gentile territory, and a deaf mute is brought to him. Christ's usual practice was to bring healing by his word, but here he makes use of certain outward signs. He takes the sick man aside, puts his finger into his ears, touches his tongue with spittle, looks up to heaven, groans and says, *Be opened.* Straightaway the ears of the man are opened, and the string of his tongue is loosed. He can hear and speak. Why did Christ use signs on this occasion? Could he not have cured the man by a word? The obvious reason for his departure from his normal practice on this occasion was the fact that here was a man who was deaf and dumb. In order to prepare him for his cure he had to use sign language.

Yet Christ had another object in mind. He was thinking of the sacred signs which his Church would use in ministering her sacraments. When he touched the ears and the tongue of the deaf-mute, saying *Be opened*, the sick man was able to hear and speak. These were visible signs which produced a visible effect. It was something similar that Christ instituted in his Church. Water is poured on a man's head, and the words *I baptize you in the name of the Father, and of the Son, and of the Holy Spirit* are pronounced, and the result is not something visible such as the healing of deafness or dumbness, but something invisible and even greater: from being a sinful creature the man becomes a child of God in whom the Holy Spirit takes up his dwelling; he puts on Christ as a garment. In giving us grace, Christ wanted to link it up with special outward and visible signs: the pouring of water in baptism, the laying on of hands in confirmation and the anointing with chrism, the bread and wine in the eucharist. He could have given us grace in a different way without special signs, but it was his declared will to join the giving of invisible grace to the visible signs instituted by him and preserved by the Church. If the Church did not have such visible signs, how could we ever have the certainty of having received grace?

Yet we can find another reason for the outward sign. Man consists of body and soul. The body acts upon the soul, and the soul upon the body. They belong together and cannot be separated permanently. Through original sin, these two parts in his nature have become opposed. The flesh lusts against the spirit, and vice versa. Christ came in order to bring these two into harmony. He did not work our redemption by abandoning sinful flesh to its fate and merely concentrating on the soul, making that holy and leading it to the Father. He took upon himself the burden and misery of human flesh, brought it to the cross, sacrificed it to the heavenly Father as a sin offering for the world, and brought it finally to salvation and glory.

(*Seasons of Grace*, 300-301)

Pius Parsch (1884-1954) was born in Moravia and became a Canon of Saint Augustine at Klosterneuburg in 1904. After ordination in 1904 he taught pastoral theology and then served as a military chaplain during World War I. Later he concentrated on biblical studies and the connection of the bible and the liturgy. He shared Pius X's concern for bringing the liturgy to the people and making it understood by them. To this purpose he devoted the many editions of liturgical texts and numerous published explanations of the liturgy that made his monastery a liturgical center of Austria, indeed of all the German-speaking lands.

Twenty-Fourth Sunday in Ordinary Time

Gospel: Mark 8:27-35

Jesus and his disciples set out for the villages around Caesarea Philippi. On the way he asked his disciples this question: "Who do people say that I am?"

Commentary: P. Tillich

*O*n the road, Jesus inquired of his disciples, *Who do people say I am? John the Baptist*, they told him, *although some say that you are Elijah, and others, that you are one of the prophets*. Why did they give him titles that elevated him above the ordinary human being? It was because they felt that behind this figure of the teaching and healing rabbi some mysterious thing was hidden. They thought that he must be the mask for one of the forerunners, who would come and prepare the new and final period of history, in which justice and peace would reign. This is what the disciples heard from the people.

And so he inquired of them, *Who do you say that I am?* Peter, in his reply, did not simply add another, and more lofty, name to the names given by the people. Peter said, *You are Christ*. In these words he expressed something which was entirely different from what the people had said. He denied that Jesus was a forerunner; he denied that somebody else should be expected. He asserted that the decisive point of history had come, and that the Christ, the bearer of the new, had come in this man Jesus, who was walking with him along a dusty village road north of Palestine.

When Peter called Jesus the Christ, the word "Christ" designated him who was to bring the liberation of Israel, the victory of God over the nations, the transformation of the human heart, and the establishment of the messianic reign of peace and justice. Through the Christ history would be fulfilled. God would become the Lord of mankind; and the earth would be changed into a place of blessedness. All this was implied in Peter's words, *You are the Christ*.

120

The greatness and the tragedy of the moment in which Peter uttered these words are visible in the reaction of Jesus: he forbade them to tell anyone about him. The messianic character of Jesus was a mystery. It did not mean to him what it meant to the people.

And he proceeded to teach them that the Son of Man must endure much suffering, must be rejected, must be killed, and after three days rise again. He spoke of this quite freely. The moment in which Peter called him the Christ, Jesus prophesied his suffering and death. He began to reveal the mystery of his messianic destiny. Jesus did not deny his messianic vocation. In the symbolic words containing the *rising after three days*, he indicated that his rejection and his death would not be a defeat, but rather the necessary steps to his becoming the Christ. He was to be the Christ only as the suffering and dying Christ.

Those who try to avoid the cross as the way, and those who hope for a Christ while rejecting the Crucified, have no knowledge of the mystery of God and of man. They are the ones who consider Jesus merely as a forerunner. They are the ones who expect others with a greater power to transform the world, others with a greater wisdom to change our hearts. But even the greatest in power and wisdom could not more fully reveal the heart of God and the heart of man than the Crucified has done already.

It is finished: of him alone can we say: he is the new reality, he is the end, he is the Messiah. To the Crucified alone can we say, *You are the Christ*.

(*Shaking the Foundations*, 142-148)

Paul Tillich (1886-1965) was born in Starzeddel, Kreis Guben, Germany, and studied at the University of Berlin (1904-1905), University of Tübingen (1905), University of Breslau (1911) where he earned his doctorate, and the University of Halle (1912). He was ordained a minister in the Lutheran Church in 1912. He taught at various universities, most notably at the Union Theological Seminary in New York from 1933-1954 and then at Harvard University and the University of Chicago Divinity School. In addition to his theological investigation he was active in helping refugees. He died in 1965.

Twenty-Fifth Sunday in Ordinary Time

Gospel: Mark 9:30-37

Jesus and his disciples came down the mountain and began to go through Galilee, but he did not want anyone to know about it. He was teaching his disciples in this vein: "The Son of Man is going to be delivered into the hands of men who will put him to death; three days after his death he will rise."

Commentary: K. Rahner

Those who do not understand the words of Christ are none other than the Twelve, his apostles, the foundation stones of the Church, Peter and the other eleven, whom he chose, whom he called, who saw his miracles, whom he gathered about him so as to make them the beginning of the new people of God. They cannot grasp the fact that he must suffer. They are not even willing to make head or tail of his declaration that in three days he will rise again.

Yet the apostles remain with Jesus. Even when they see that they do not understand what is going on, they remain steadfast. They are faithful. They are patient. They make Jesus, as it were, an advance payment of confidence and time, giving him a chance to grow in their hearts. And we must add that God bears with them. Though their hearts are darkened, though they do not understand, though in their inertia they hardly want to understand, they remain undergird by God's mercy, his faithfulness, his providence, and his love. Mystery uncomprehended stands between them and the Lord, yet does not separate them. Neither abandons the other. Each cleaves to the other, because God loves and is faithful, because man realizes that though he may not understand the mystery, God and God's grace are only to be found where that mystery is.

Is there a lesson here for our own life? If we compare all that we can grasp and understand, all that is clear and straightforward in our lives, with the obscure and the baffling, the hidden and uncomprehended, the mysterious and unspeakable, then we seem to see a tiny candle burning in the midst of endless darkness. How can it be otherwise so long as we are here making our way among parabolic shadows, still on pilgrimage toward the everlasting light, the unapproachable light that only God can be?

Would it not be folly to expect everything to be intelligible, or to accept no more than we can understand? The incomprehensible must lay hold on us, for only then shall we be open to God the infinite, and only if we are that, have we the hope and the promise that we shall find everything.

(Biblical Homilies, 62-64)

Karl Rahner, S.J. (1901-1984), a Swabian by birth, entered the Society of Jesus in 1922 and was ordained ten years later. After completing his studies at Freiburg and Innsbruck he was appointed to the theological faculty of Innsbruck in 1936. In 1949 he became a professor of dogmatic theology and in 1964 was appointed to a professorship in Munich. As a theological editor his name is associated with Denziger's *Enchiridion Symbolorum* and also with the *Lexikon für Theologie und Kirche* and *Sacramentum Mundi*. He was a peritus at Vatican II and the many volumes of *Theological Investigations* testify to his tireless labor as a theologian. Etienne Gilson drew attention to Rahner's "combination of intellectual modesty and audacity." A theologian of penetrating insight, he was also without doubt a man of God.

Twenty-Sixth Sunday in Ordinary Time

Gospel: Mark 9:38-43.45.47-48 John said to Jesus: "Teacher, we saw a man using your name to expel demons and we tried to stop him because he is not of our company."

Commentary: H. Lacordaire

The one who loves God is a living member of the Church, under whatever sky he may be hidden and in whatever age he lives. "Two loves have made two cities," said Saint Augustine: the love of this world has made the city of men, the love of God has made the city of God. And of this last-named love, Jesus Christ is the Father. From the beginning of the world he was sacrificed in advance for us; in his extreme suffering he has moved our feelings that are too cold and too guilty to turn to God naturally. It is true that not all men know the origin of the flame that consumes them. Some of them cannot call on the name of Jesus Christ, because Jesus Christ has never been uttered to them. Obscure victims of the saving cross, they were not led to the foot of Calvary from their birth; they have not seen there God-become-man in the agony which he suffered for their salvation. But a drop of this blood has sought them through invisible tracks, bringing to their blood the fragrance of eternal life, and they have responded to the mute appeal of charity with a silent groan.

The Church is not only what it seems to us. It is not only in this visible building where everything is history, hierarchy, authenticity, virtues and shining miracles; it is also in the half-light, in the blur of shadows, in what has neither form nor memory, saintliness lost to men's sight but not to that of the angels, and which, presenting nothing to the legitimate pride of truth, yet makes for it an underground foundation and support. There is not a single soul, moreover, not even the most wellknown, that has not an impenetrable sanctuary and which does not offer to God in this holy of holies a hidden incense which counts this world's show as nothing but yet weighs in the glory of the next. Love, which is the foundation of the Church, is the most evasive of living fluids, and if the eye of men has never yet been able to detect in the swift current of his nerves the immortal substance which impels them, how much less is he aware of the ways taken by Divine Love?

Wherever the love of God is, there is Jesus Christ; wherever Jesus Christ is, the Church is there with him; and if it is true that every Christian should join the body of the Church as soon as he becomes aware of its existence, it is certain that insuperable ignorance puts him out of reach of this law, to leave him under the direct rule of Jesus Christ, Leader and Sovereign Head of all Christianity. The Church has therefore an extension that no human eye could compass, and those who confront us with the boundaries which it appears to have in their eyes have no idea of the twofold radiance which is in its nature, and which raises up souls to it in East and West, in the world of both the setting and the rising sun.

(*Mélanges*, IX, 328-331)

Henri Lacordaire, O.P. (1802-1861), a lawyer full of prospects, presented himself at Saint-Sulpice in 1824 and was ordained a priest in 1827. Involved with Lamennais in modernism, he submitted himself completely to the Roman Magisterium. Entering the Order of Preachers, he took the name Dominic and dedicated himself to the renewal of the Dominicans in France. His conferences at Notre Dame have made him famous. A rare oratorical talent, an extremely fine sensitivity, as well as a kind of passion in regard to the realities of the faith, distinguishes this preacher who felt himself impelled by the very love of Christ to proclaim the word in season and out of season.

Twenty-Seventh Sunday in Ordinary Time

Gospel: Mark 10:2-16

Some Pharisees came up and as a test began to ask Jesus whether it was permissible for a husband to divorce his wife.

Commentary: W. Harrington

New Testament teaching on divorce has come under special scrutiny in recent times and this passage from Saint Mark figures prominently in all studies of the subject. Almost all contemporary exegetes and theologians perceive that Jesus seeks to restore marriage to the original form God intends it to have. Husband and wife are "two in one flesh," implying a covenant bond between persons far transcending physical union. Love, seeking only the good of the beloved, is the true marriage bond; love is, or should be, the call impelling a man to leave his father and his mother and to cleave in life-long union to his wife. Jesus prohibited divorce under the assumption that the marriage involved is a real marriage.

Implicitly, then, the current trend is centered not so much on divorce as on marriage, and what marriage should ideally be. The measure of this is the perfect spousal love that is taught in Ephesians 5. This love is but one vital aspect of the entire "one commandment" of love which Jesus has given to us. For those who are believers the solution to marriage difficulties is not desertion but forgiveness and a rekindling of love. The fact remains that Christians, no less than others, are human and frail. The entire question of divorce seems to call for great realism in looking at individual persons and the concrete situations in which they find themselves. It calls for an awareness of the greatest "realism" of all, a reality surpassing the ideal of irrevocable unity in marriage. And this is the real love which Jesus himself has for each of us. "He understands our humanness," for we have not a high priest who is unable to sympathize with our weaknesses but one who in every respect has been tempted as we are, yet without sinning, and he desires to give us the freedom in which to share his love. He is the truth who sets us free: in him rests the ultimate union of "two in one flesh."

(Saint Mark, 152-153)

Wilfrid J. Harrington, O.P., a graduate of the École Biblique in Jerusalem, is a native of Ireland. He has lectured widely and has written books and articles on biblical subjects.

Twenty-Eighth Sunday in Ordinary Time

Gospel: Mark 10:17-30

As Jesus was setting out on a journey a man came running up, knelt down before him and asked, "Good Teacher, what must I do to share in everlasting life?"

Commentary: S. Kierkegaard

To follow Christ means denying one's self, and hence it means *walking the same way* as Christ walked in the humble form of a servant — needy, forsaken, mocked, not loving worldliness and not loved by the worldly-minded. Consequently it means to *walk alone*, for he who in self-abnegation renounces the world and all that is the world's, forsakes every relationship which otherwise tempts and holds captive, so that he "neither attends to his fields, nor to bargaining, nor to getting married"; he who, if it becomes necessary, certainly does not love his father or mother or sister or brother less than before, but loves Christ so much more that he may be said to hate those others: he walks absolutely alone, alone in the whole world. Moreover, in the crucial pressure of life, it seems a difficult, an impossible thing to live in such a way; impossible even to decide whether anyone actually does live this way. But let us not forget that it is eternity which is to judge how the task was performed, and that the earnestness of eternity will impose the silence of diffidence concerning all the worldliness which is incessantly talked about in the world.

For in eternity you will not be asked how great a fortune you *left behind you*—your *posterity* will ask about that. You will not be asked how many battles you won, how clever you were, how powerful an influence you had exerted—that becomes your *posthumous* fame in the future. No, eternity will not ask about what *worldly* possessions you left *behind* you in the world. But it will ask you what treasure you have accumulated in heaven; how often you have won the victory over your own temper; what self-control you have exercised over yourself, or whether you have been a slave;

how many times you have mastered yourself in self-denial, or whether you never have done so; how often in self-abnegation you have been willing to sacrifice for a good cause, or whether you never have been willing; how frequently in self-abnegation you have forgiven your enemy, whether indeed seven times or seventy times seven; how frequently in self-abnegation you have borne injuries patiently; what you have suffered, not for your own sake, for the sake of your own selfish purposes, but what in self-abnegation you have suffered for God's sake.

And he who will ask you, the Judge, from whose judgment you cannot appeal to any higher judgment, he was not a commander who ruled over kingdoms and countries, with whom you might talk of your earthly achievements; his kingdom was not exactly of this world. He was not a man clothed in purple, with whom you might associate in distinguished company, for he wore the purple only as an insult. He did not wield a powerful influence, so that he might wish to be initiated into your worldly secrets, for he was so despised that the distinguished man dared seek him only in the secrecy of night. Oh, it is always a comfort to foregather with the like-minded; if one is cowardly, then not to have to be brought before a court-martial; if one is selfish and worldly-minded, then not to have to be judged by the self-denying. And this Judge not only knows what self-denial is, he not only knows how to judge so that no irregularity can conceal itself; no, his presence is the judgment which causes all things to turn pale and become silent, that which to worldliness looked so good out in the world, which was heard and seen with admiration. His presence is the judgment, for he was self-denial. He who was equal with God took on the humble form of a servant.

(*The Gospel of Suffering*, 11-13)

Søren Kierkegaard (1813-1855) resided all his life in the large family dwelling in central Copenhagen, where he was prominent as a literary figure. An unhappy love affair and quarrels with other writers and, in his last years, with the Church — all documented in lengthy journals — make up the story of his life. With a degree in theology, he put off taking orders (Lutheran); still, an overriding sense of what the gospel can mean to those who embrace it with faith and love led him to sandwich in between his various poetical and philosophical writings a number of spiritual books.

Twenty-Ninth Sunday
in Ordinary Time

Gospel: Mark 10:35-45

Zebedee's sons, James and John, approached Jesus. "Teacher," they said, "we want you to grant our request."

Commentary: A. de Orozco

Whoever desires to be greater among you, let him be your minister. And whoever desires to be first among you will be your servant. O heavenly philosophy! O divinely marvelous teaching! Would that ecclesiastics and all religious men would write it deep in their hearts. Does anyone reach such a state of madness that, knowing himself to be free, he nonetheless desires to be a slave and strives with all his strength to become one? And yet there are those who strive to be over others, as the Lord implies when he says: *Whoever desires to be first among you will be your servant.* I also recall that the apostle said: *Whoever desires the office of bishop desires a good work.* But in fact episcopate is the name of a burden, not an honor, as both Saint Augustine and Saint Thomas finely explain. Chrysostom, followed by Saint Basil, says that it is good to desire a good work, but vanity to seek the first place. The same thought is implicit in the fact that our Supreme Pontiff calls himself, not lord, but servant of the servants of Christ.

Finally, in order that his disciples may better learn this serious lesson, Jesus offers himself as a wonderful example, when he says: *The Son of Man came not to be served but to serve and to give his life as a ransom for the many.* This is a brilliantly clear mirror which it befits pastors of the Church to have always and everywhere before their eyes, so that they may be humble and poor in spirit. He who certainly knew well how tyrannical ambition can become and what a loss it can inflict on angels and human beings, came humbly from heaven in order to tear down the tower of Babel by the strength of his humility. *Though he was in the form of God, he did not think of equality of God as something to be snatched at, but he emptied himself and took the form of a slave*, in order to transport us to the heavenly realms above.

Beloved, I plead with you to contemplate with the whole power of your mind the humiliating death Christ died and to follow in his steps. Do not desire first place in this life, as the two apostles did, for like the grass of the field it quickly withers and disappears, as Isaiah warns us. Let us drink the Lord's cup and freely carry his cross, while crying out with David: *What return shall I make to the Lord for all that he has given to me? I will take the cup of salvation and call upon the name of the Lord. For precious in the sight of the Lord is the death of his holy ones.* And this, according to Blessed Jerome, is what it means to drink the "chalice of the Lord": to be dead to our desires and the world and to lead an innocent life with Christ, who has made this promise: *To the one who overcomes as I have overcome I will give to sit on my throne as I sit on the throne of my Father.* To him be glory and honor through endless ages. Amen.

(Wednesday, Second Week of Lent, Sermon 10, *Opera omnia* I,
294-295)

Alonso de Orozco, O.S.A. (1500-1591) studied at the University of Salamanca before entering the Augustinian novitiate there. His main apostolates in the Order were preaching and writing, and although he was chosen as royal preacher at the Spanish court, he preferred to speak to poor and simple people. His religious life was marked by a spirit of fraternity, gospel simplicity, and moderation in speech. As an ascetic and great mystic, he suffered crisis and spiritual aridity from 1522 to 1551. He was beatified by Pope Leo XIII in 1882.

Thirtieth Sunday in Ordinary Time

Gospel: Mark 10:46-52

As Jesus was leaving Jericho with his disciples and a sizable crowd, there was a blind beggar Bartimaeus ("son of Timaeus") sitting by the roadside. On hearing that it was Jesus of Nazareth, he began to call out, "Jesus, Son of David, have pity on me!"

Commentary: A. Bloom

I believe that one of the reasons which prevent us from being truly ourselves and finding our own way is that we do not realize the extent to which we are blind! If only we knew that we were blind, how eagerly would we seek healing: we should seek it, as Bartimaeus probably did, from men, doctors, priests, healers; and then, having lost all hope "in princes, in the sons of men in whom there is no salvation," we might, perhaps, turn to God. But the tragedy is that we do not realize our blindness: too many things leap to our eyes for us to be aware of the invisible to which we are blind.

Blinded by the world of things we forget that it does not match the depth of which man is capable. Man is both small and great. When we think of ourselves in an ever-expanding universe—immeasurably big or infinitely small—we see ourselves as a speck of dust, transient, frail, of no account; but when we turn inward we discover that nothing in this immensity is great enough to fill us to the brim—the whole created world falls like a grain of sand into the depth of our being: we are too vast for it to fill or fulfill us. God alone, who has made us for himself, on his scale, can do that.

The world of things has an opacity, a density, weight and volume, but it has no depth. We can always penetrate to the heart of things, and when we have reached their deepest point, it is a terminal point, there is no way through to infinity: the center of a sphere is its innermost point but if we try to go beyond that we return to the surface at the antipodes. But holy scripture speaks of the depth of the human heart. It is not a depth that can be measured; its very nature is immensity, it goes beyond all bounds of measurement. This depth is rooted in the immensity of God himself. It is only when we have understood the difference between a presence that asserts itself and a presence we have to seek because we sense it in our hearts, when we have understood the difference between the heavy, opaque density of the world around us and the human profundity which only God can fill—it is only then that we can begin our search in the knowledge that we are blind, blinded by the visible which prevents us grasping the invisible.

To be blind to the invisible, to be aware only of the tangible world, is to be on the outside of the fullness of knowledge, outside the experience of total reality which is the world in God and God at the heart of the world. The blind man Bartimaeus was painfully aware of this because owing to his physical blindness, the visible world escaped him. He could cry out to the Lord in utter despair, with all the desperate hope he felt when salvation was passing him by, because he felt himself cut off. The reason why all too often we cannot call to God in this way is that we do not realize how much we are cut off by being blind to the total vision of the world—a vision which could afford complete reality to the visible world itself. If only we could learn to be blind to the visible in order to see beyond, in depth, the invisible, in and around us, penetrating all things with its presence!

(Meditations — A Spiritual Journey, 25-29)

Anthony Bloom (1914-), Metropolitan of Sourozh, born Andrew Borisovich Bloom in Lausanne, Switzerland, was educated at the Sorbonne, became a doctor of medicine before taking monastic vows in 1943 and became a priest of the Russian Orthodox Church in Paris in 1948. In 1960 he was ordained archbishop of Sourozh and then became in 1965 Metropolitan and Patriarch of Moscow and All Russia in Western Europe. He lectured in various parts of the world and authored many books on prayer and the spiritual life.

Thirty-First Sunday in Ordinary Time

Gospel: Mark 12:28-34

One of the scribes came up to Jesus, and asked him, "Which is the first of all the commandments?"

Commentary: F. de Sales

Because God created us in his own image and likeness, he ordained that our love for one another should be in the image and likeness of the love we owe him, our God. He said: You must love the Lord your God with your whole heart. This is the first and greatest commandment. The second is like it: You must love your neighbor as yourself.

What is our reason for loving God? God himself is the reason we love him; we love him because he is the supreme and infinite goodness. What is our reason for loving ourselves? Surely because we are the image and likeness of God. And since all men and women possess this same dignity we love them as ourselves, that is, as holy and living images of the Godhead. It is as such that we belong to God through a kinship so close and a dependence so lovable that he does not hesitate to call himself our Father, and to name us his children. It is as such that we are capable of being united to him in the fruition of his sovereign goodness and joy. It is as such that we receive his grace and that our spirits are associated with his most Holy Spirit and rendered, in a sense, *sharers in the divine nature.*

So it is then that the same charity produces together acts of the love of God and of our neighbor. As Jacob saw that the same ladder touching heaven and earth was used by the angels both for ascending and descending, so we can be sure that the same charity cherishes both God and our neighbor, raising us even to spiritual union with God, and bringing us back to loving companionship with our neighbors. It must always be understood, however, that we love our neighbors for this reason, that they are made in the image and likeness of God, created to communicate in his goodness, share in his grace, and rejoice in his glory.

To have a Christian love for our neighbors is to love God in them, or them in God; it is to cherish God alone for his own sake, and his creatures for love of him. When we look upon our neighbors, created in the image and likeness of God, should we not say to each other: "Look at these people he has made — are they not like their Maker?" Should we not be drawn irresistibly toward them, embrace them, and be moved to tears for love of them? Should we not call down upon them a hundred thousand blessings? And why? For love of them? No indeed, since we cannot be sure whether, of themselves, they are worthy of love or hate. Then why? For love of God, who created them in his own image and likeness, and so are capable of sharing in his goodness, grace, and glory; for love of God, I say, unto whom they exist, from whom they exist, through whom they exist, in whom they exist, for whom they exist, and whom they resemble in a very special manner.

This is why divine love not only repeatedly commands us to love our neighbors, but also itself produces this love and pours it out into our hearts, since they bear its own image and likeness; for just as we are the image of God, so our holy love for one another is the true image of our heavenly love for God.

(*Treatise on the Love of God*, 193-195)

Francis de Sales (1567-1622), born near Annecy, France, from early childhood evinced signs of his vocation to the priestly apostolate. On becoming a priest after his studies at Paris and Padua, he was at first provost of the Church of Geneva and preached to the inhabitants of Chablais to lead them back to Catholicism. In 1602, he was elevated to the episcopal see of Geneva. Under his direction, Saint Jane Frances de Chantal founded the Order of the Visitation. He died in one of the monasteries of that Order, at Lyons, in 1622. His life and writings were pervaded by a gentleness, affability, love, and delightful good fellowship but they hid an explosive temperament which was able to remain calm by being open to the grace of God.

Thirty-Second Sunday in Ordinary Time

Gospel: Mark 12:38-44

In the course of his teaching Jesus said: "Be on guard against the scribes, who like to parade around in their robes and accept marks of respect in public, front seats in the synagogues, and places of honor at banquets."

Commentary: R. Schnackenburg

*I*n the temple Court of the Women was a hall (the treasury) with thirteen trumpet-shaped receptacles for money offerings for various purposes, including voluntary gifts without special destination. Visitors to the temple did not insert the money themselves as we do into collection boxes, but handed it to the priests who put it in the receptacles as the donor decided. This explains how Jesus could see what the poor widow gave. She named the amount and its purpose to the priest and Jesus could hear her. In the circumstances she probably brought her very modest contribution as a voluntary gift without special destination, for which the thirteenth receptacle was reserved. This money was used to provide burnt offerings. The woman wanted only to do something for the glory of God. Alms for the poor were handed in elsewhere, or collected in a box.

The lesson for the disciples and consequently to the later community is plain. True piety is devotion to God; it means placing oneself totally at his disposal. This woman does not give of her superfluity, but out of her poverty and need. She gave away all that she had, perhaps (from the Greek expression) all that she had to live on that day. The *two* smallest Jewish coins show that she could still have reserved something for herself, but in fact she gave God everything and thereby gave herself. A person of this stamp will not fail to notice others in distress and share their last crust with them if need be. The widow loves God "with all her strength," which in the Jewish interpretation also meant with her whole earthly "property," all her possessions. There are non-Christian examples of high esteem for the inner disposition that prompts an action rather than the size of the gift or the mere scale of what is done. The Christian element can be discerned in the light of the great commandment, when a person gives himself lovingly in sacrifice to God, and, for his sake, to humanity.

(*New Testament for Spiritual Reading*, volume 2, 89-90)

Rudolf Schnackenburg (1914-), born in Kathewicz, Germany, studied theology at the University of Brelayn and New Testament exegesis at the University of Munich. After ordination he taught in the University of Dillingen (1952-1955), the University of Bamberg (1955-1957), and from 1957 at the University of Würzburg. He was involved in ecumenical work and lectured in the United States.

Thirty-Third Sunday in Ordinary Time

Gospel: Mark 13:24-32

Jesus said to his disciples: "During that period after trials of every sort the sun will be darkened, the moon will not shed its light, stars will fall out of the skies, and the heavenly hosts will be shaken."

Commentary: P. T. de Chardin

One day, the gospel tells us, the tension gradually accumulating between humanity and God will touch the limits prescribed by the possibilities of the world. And then will come the end. Then the presence of Christ, which has been silently accruing in all things, will suddenly be revealed — like a flash of light from pole to pole. Creaking through all the barriers within which the veil of matter has seemingly kept it confined, it will invade the face of the earth. Like lightning, like a conflagration, like a flood, the attraction exerted by the Son of Man will lay hold of all the whirling elements in the universe to reunite them or subject them to his body.

As the gospel warns us, it would be vain to speculate as to the hour and the modalities of this formidable event. But we have to *expect* it. Expectation — that is perhaps the supreme Christian function and the most distinctive characteristic of our religion. Historically speaking, that expectation has never ceased to guide the progress of our faith like a torch. The Israelites were constantly expectant, and the first Christians too. Christmas, which might have been thought to turn our gaze toward the past, has only fixed it further in the future. The Messiah, who appeared for a moment in our midst, only allowed himself to be seen and touched for a moment before vanishing again, more luminous and ineffable than ever, into the depths of the future. He came. Yet now we must expect him. Successors to Israel, we Christians have been charged with keeping the flame of desire ever alive in the world. Only twenty centuries have passed since the Ascension. What have we made of our expectancy? We persist in saying that we keep vigil in expectation of the Master. But in reality we should have to admit, if we are sincere, that we no longer expect anything.

The flame must be revived at all costs. At all costs we must renew in ourselves the desire and the hope for the great Coming. But the expectation cannot remain alive unless it is incarnate. What body shall we give to ours today? That of a *totally human* hope. Let us look at the earth around us. Mankind is visibly passing through a crisis of growth; it is becoming dimly aware of its shortcomings and its capacities; it has a sense of premonition and of expectation. Those of us who are disciples of Christ must not hesitate to harness this force, which needs us and which we need. On the contrary, under pain of allowing it to be lost and of perishing ourselves, we should share those aspirations, in essence religious, which make the men of today feel so strongly the immensity of the world, the greatness of the mind, and the sacred value of each truth. The progress of the universe, and in particular of the human universe, does not take place in competition with God, nor does it squander energies that we rightly owe to him. The greater man becomes, the more humanity becomes united, with consciousness of its potentialities, the more beautiful creation will be, the more perfect adoration will become, and the more Christ will find a body worthy of resurrection.

(*Le Milieu Divin*, epilogue)

Pierre Teilhard de Chardin (1881-1955), a priest of the Society of Jesus, was a scientist and theologian of unparalleled insight. Enlightened by a passionate love of God immanent in all things, and taught by a lifetime's meticulous study of geology, biology, and paleontology, he was brought to a vision of the universe's evolution toward its rebirth and transformation in a union of love with Christ, its "Omega-Point." This he explored in many of his writings, notably *Le Milieu Divin* and *The Phenomenon of Man*. His life was one with his teaching, absorbed in adoration, deeply aware of God's presence at all times.

Christ the King
Thirty-Fourth Sunday in Ordinary Time

Gospel: John 18:33-37   Pilate said to Jesus: "Are you the king of the Jews?"

Commentary: A. Boultwood

The last Sunday of the liturgical year is dedicated by the Church to the feast of Christ the King. The royal title is perhaps not altogether natural to modern minds, and some others might be more appealing. Yet Jesus himself did not deny his kingship, even though he always frustrated the attempts of the crowds to lead him to any worldly kingdom. In the noblest and truest sense of all, he is king of all his Father's creation, for in Jesus all things find their purpose, salvation, and fulfillment. The incarnate Son is the only Mediator in the plan of divine love, by which all creation attains its true end and comes to the Father.

At the birth of this Jesus we sang the old hymn asking "What child is this?" and Christian faith and devotion answered "This, this is Christ the King." As this same Jesus was dying on the cross, Pilate set above his head the ironic sign, more to mock the Jews than the Crucified: *Jesus of Nazareth, King of the Jews.* What king is this? Christian faith answers more fervently than ever that this is indeed the true King, whose cross wins redemption for sinners, and whose death wins victory over all the powers of death.

Christ gained his victory and established his kingdom not through the power of worldly success but through a love stronger than all the powers of this world. His authority was from above, from his perfect union with the Father's will. Yet his kingship was very truly in this world, for he won his redeeming victory by entering completely into the human condition, including its suffering and death. In Jesus there was thus achieved a perfect but mysterious solution to the painful division in our nature. Through him divine goodness truly penetrates our world, and if it is willingly received it totally transforms creation so that now all is grace.

Humans are called and enabled to live not to sin but to God, in true newness of life. This is the universal kingship of Christ; everything is now renewed and glorified in him, nothing is left unredeemable: *Take courage, I have overcome the world* (John 16:33).

Christ held his kingship in two ways. As the only-begotten Son of the Father, it was his by right, and in his humanity he gained it by the perfect oblation of his loving obedience on the cross, thus restoring the whole world to the Father. Correspondingly, our own heritage in the kingdom of Christ is held in two ways. First, by the free gift of our Father in heaven, and secondly by our following the ways of Christ's sacrificial kingship in this life, sharing his acceptance of the conditions of this world, its suffering and mortality, and transforming these by that self-giving which he filled with grace. Therefore all his followers in the royal priesthood must always form a serving, suffering, loving Church. We inherit the kingship of Jesus by fulfilling the mystery of his blessed Passion, death, and resurrection in the witness of our own personal life. In this way we *fill up what is lacking in the sufferings of Christ for the sake of his body the Church*, and we share in his royal mission of redemption till the end of time. Christ's kingship truly continues on earth in us; this is both the wonderful dignity and the tremendous responsibility of our Christian vocation.

(*Christ in Us*, 137-138)

Alban Boultwood (1911-) was born in Stamford, Connecticut, entered the Benedictine Order in 1929 and was ordained a priest in 1939. He studied at Collegio Sant' Anselmo in Rome and also at the University of Edinburgh. He was abbot of Saint Anselm Abbey, Washington DC, from 1961-1975.

Presentation of the Lord

Gospel: Luke 2:22-40   When the day came to purify them according to the law of Moses, the couple brought Jesus up to Jerusalem so that he could be presented to the Lord.

Commentary: John Paul II

*F*orty days after the nativity the Church celebrates an event full of spiritual significance. On that day the Son of God, as a tiny child of poor parents, born in a rough stable in Bethlehem, was carried to the temple in Jerusalem. This was his own temple, the temple of the living God, but he came to it not as the Lord but as one under the law. For the poor the law prescribed that forty days after the birth of the firstborn two turtle-doves or two young pigeons must be offered in sacrifice, as a sign that the child was consecrated to the Lord.

The message which the Spirit of God allowed the old man Simeon to sense and express so wonderfully was implicitly in the event itself, in this first encounter between the Messiah and his temple. On seeing the child, Simeon begins to utter words that are not of human provenance. He prophesies, prompted by the Holy Spirit; he speaks with the voice of God, the God for whom the temple was built and who is its rightful master.

Simeon's words begin, in what the liturgy calls the Song, by bearing witness to the light, and in so doing they ante-date by thirty years the witness borne by John the Baptist. They end, on the other hand, by bearing the first witness to the cross, in which contradiction of Jesus, the Christ, is to find tangible expression. The cost of the cross was shared by the mother, whose soul—according to Simeon's words—was to be pierced by a sword, *so that the thoughts of many hearts may be laid bare.*

Chronologically the presentation of Jesus in the temple is linked with the nativity, but in its significance it belongs with the mystery of the pasch. It is the first of the events which clearly reveal the messianic status of the newborn child. With him are linked the fall and the rising of many in the old Israel and also the new. On him the future of humankind depends. It is he who is the true Lord of the ages to come. His reign begins when the temple sacrifice is offered in accordance with the law, and it attains full realization through the sacrifice on the cross, offered in accordance with an eternal plan of love.

(*Sign of Contradiction,* 40-41)

John Paul II (1920-), born Karol Wojtyla, was ordained a priest in 1946, a bishop in 1958, made a cardinal in 1967, and elected pope in 1978. Hewn from the colossus of Polish Catholicism, formed by the discipline of study and manual labor, his physical, moral, and intellectual strength has been the rock on which the grace of God has built up the Church during a period of consolidation after Vatican II. His particular insights into the human condition, shaped by his interest in the theater, his gifts for poetry and playwriting, and his study of personalist philosophy, have contributed much to the teaching of the Church.

Saints Peter and Paul

Gospel: Matthew 16:13-19

When Jesus had appeared to his disciples and had eaten with them, he said to Simon Peter, "Simon, son of John, do you love me more than these?" "Yes, Lord," Peter said, "you know that I love you." At which Jesus said, "Feed my lambs."

Commentary: J. Bonsirven

*I*n Palestine, the only solid foundation people knew was rock—*Kepha* in Aramaic. Simon, son of John, was to be this foundation. By this metaphor, an exalted rank in the Church, the primacy, was assigned to Peter, and its rights and prerogatives would become apparent as they were exercised. Paul, when he speaks of Christ as the chief cornerstone in the edifice of the Church, does not hesitate to call the apostles and the prophets the foundation on which the Church is built. There are some words of his which bear witness to the fact that the early Christians called Simon *Kepha* and acknowledged that his was a position of real primacy.

This was the first time Jesus mentioned his Church. Like Christ himself and all that he was doing, the Church was to be the target for the attacks of hostile powers represented here by "the gates of Hades," Hades being thought of then as the abode of the wicked, while in poetic style the gates designated a fortress. The satanic powers would not prevail against either the society or the rock which upheld it. The reign of God continued to triumph over the devil. In fact, the phrases which follow seem to identify the Church with the reign of God; Jesus has the power of a ruler in both of them. He appointed Peter Grand Vizier, the governor of the kingdom. His extensive power is symbolized by the keys, which the master of the house withdrew and handed over to his true servant. This authority is also indicated by the power to "bind and loose," words used in the rabbinical vocabulary to designate the power of the judiciary and the legislature.

The primacy of Peter is once again implied in the promise made to him on the eve of the passion. This event is compared with the act of sifting corn; only the good grain remains in the riddle: all the rest, straw, bad grain, soil, is thrown out. In the same way, the faith of the apostles was to be violently disturbed by the great ordeal. Their leader would not be overcome completely, and once he had returned to his original loyalty, would strengthen his brethren and direct them in their faith.

Peter was confirmed in his dignity later by our Lord after his resurrection—it was after his triumph that the Church was to show signs of autonomous life. We know the dialogue which was exchanged on the banks of the Sea of Tiberias amid the splendor of the rising sun. The Master wanted to make it clear to Simon by his thrice-repeated question that his office demanded a greater degree of love: the leader, more than anyone, must share the infinite charity of the supreme head. His official title was "shepherd." God called himself the shepherd of his people and gave the same title to the prophets, and especially to the Messiah. Jesus also described himself as the "good shepherd," proving his love for his flock by the sacrifice of his life. He made Peter his colleague and deputy in this pastoral ministry, which included the care and direction of the faithful.

(*The Theology of the New Testament,* 66-69)

Joseph Bonsirven (1880-1958), after his education and ordination at the Sulpician seminary in Paris, was assigned to teach scripture at the major seminary of Albi. In 1906 he studied at the École Biblique under Père Lagrange; in 1909 he received his licentiate in sacred scripture from the Pontifical Biblical Commission. The following year his doctoral thesis on rabbinic eschatology was not accepted, and he was forbidden to teach scripture. Bonsirven humbly accepted the decision and returned to his diocese for pastoral work, which was interrupted by service and subsequent imprisonment in World War I. While a prisoner of war, he was appointed by Benedict XV to teach dogmatic theology and scripture to imprisoned seminarians. After the war he joined the Society of Jesus and returned to teaching New Testament exegesis in France and then in Rome at the Biblical Institute.

Transfiguration of the Lord

Gospel: Matthew 17:1-9

Jesus took Peter, James, and his brother John and led them up a high mountain by themselves. He was transfigured before their eyes. His face became as dazzling as the sun, his clothes as radiant as light.

Commentary: J. Corbon

What took place in this unexpected event? Why did the Incomprehensible One allow his "elusive beauty" to be glimpsed for a moment in the body of the world? Two certainties can serve us as guides. First, the change, or, to transliterate the Greek word, the "metamorphosis," was not a change in Jesus. The gospel text and the unanimous interpretation of the Fathers are clear: Christ "was transfigured, not by acquiring what he was not but by manifesting to his disciples what he in fact was; he opened their eyes and gave these blind men sight." The change is on the side of the disciples. The second certainty confirms this point: the purpose of the transfiguration, like everything else in the economy that is revealed in the Bible, is the salvation of human beings. As in the burning bush, so here the Word "allows" the light of his divinity "to be seen" in his body, in order to communicate not knowledge but life and salvation; he reveals himself by giving himself and he gives himself in order to transform us into himself.

But if it be permissible to take off the sandals of curiosity and inquisitive gnosis and draw near to the mystery, we may ask: Why did Jesus choose this particular moment, these two witnesses and these three apostles? What was he, the Son—so passionately in love with the Father and so passionately concerned for us—experiencing in his heart? A few days before Peter had already been given an interior enlightenment and had acknowledged Jesus as the Christ of God. Jesus had then begun to lift the veil from the not far distant ending of his life: he had to suffer, be put to death, and be raised from the dead. It is between this first prediction and the second that he undertakes to ascend the mountain. The reason for the transfiguration can be glimpsed, therefore, in what the evangelists do not say: having finished the instruction preparatory to his own Pasch, Jesus is determined to advance to its accomplishment. With the whole of his being, the whole of his "body," he is committed to the loving will of the Father; he accepts that will without reservation. From now on, everything, up to and including the final struggle at which the same three disciples will be invited to be present, will be an expression of his unconditional "Yes" to the Father's love.

We must certainly enter into this mystery of committed love if we are to understand that the transfiguration is not an impossible unveiling of the light of the Word to the eyes of the apostles, but rather a moment of intensity in which the entire being of Jesus is utterly united with the compassion of the Father. During these decisive days of his life he becomes transparent to the light of the love of the One who gives himself to human beings for their salvation. The radiance of the light in the suffering body of Jesus is as it were the thrill experienced by the Father in response to the total self-giving of his only Son. This explains the voice that pierces through the cloud: "This is my Son, the Beloved; he enjoys my favor. Listen to him" (Mt 17:5).

(The Wellspring of Worship, 60-61)

Jean Corbon is a member of the Dominican community of Beirut and author of the book *L'Église des Arabes*. His whole thrust in writing on liturgy is to rediscover its meaning and to understand how the whole of life finds itself transformed.

Assumption of Mary

Gospel: Luke 9:39-56   Mary set out, proceeding in haste into the hill country to a town of Judah, where she entered Zechariah's house and greeted Elizabeth.

Commentary: L. Bouyer

Mary should be looked on as the living pledge of Christ's promises to the Church: that where he is, we also shall be; then the glory given him by the Father he will give to us, as he received it.

Consequently, it goes without saying that Mary's Assumption is, by no means, a kind of apotheosis dispensing her from the common human destiny, any more than the Immaculate Conception was an abnormal privilege designed to emancipate her from the conditions of human life. But, as Mary, by the grace of redemption brought by her Son, a grace to which, in opening herself, she opened the whole of humankind, was the first to be saved, and that more perfectly than any other person, as regards sin, so she is seen as saved the first and more perfectly than anyone else, as regards death, the result of sin. Her Immaculate Conception was the pledge of the perfect and wholly virginal purity to which, one day, the creature, sullied by sin, has to attain, in order to become the Spouse of Christ. Likewise, her Assumption is the pledge of the glory Christ will give to his spouse, as he has already given it to his mother. As John says: *It has not yet appeared what we shall be. We know that, when he shall appear, we shall be like to him, because we shall see him as he is.* For Mary, this condition is already realized. Her perfect faith passed, as it were, without any intermediate stage to sight. In the mother of Christ and our mother, we are given the pledge of his promise; seeing him as she sees him, we shall be like to her, who is already like to him. As Paul says: *We shall be taken up together to meet Christ, and so we shall always be with the Lord.*

How, then, are we to represent, as far as is possible, this state of glory, of eschatology already realized, to which Mary has entered in the train of her Son?

Christ's ascension does not mean that he has left us to our present condition, since he has gone only to prepare a place for us, that where he is we also may be; no more does Mary's assumption mean her separation from us. As her son is represented in the letter to the Hebrews as *always living to intercede for us*, so she remains, as the constant belief of the Church assures us, at his side, the interceder par excellence. Already her blessedness is perfect, present, as she is, with God who has placed in her his delight. But, more than ever, the contemplative prayer which raises her above the angels, in the bliss of an eternal eucharist, carries an irresistible intercession, on her part, that sinners, all of us countless children of hers, may come to be united to her in her Son.

(The Seat of Wisdom, 202-203)

Louis Bouyer (1913-), born of Protestant parents, became a Lutheran minister until, as he says, "his profound studies into the nature of Protestantism as a genuinely spiritual movement led him gradually to the recognition that Catholicism was the only Church in which the positive elements of the Reformation could be exercised." He became a priest of the French Oratory and professor of spiritual theology at the Institut Catholique in Paris. He has written extensively on both ecumenism and liturgy.

Triumph of the Holy Cross

Gospel: John 3:13-17

No one has gone up to heaven except the one who came down from there—the Son of Man. Just as Moses lifted up the serpent in the desert, so must the Son of Man be lifted up, that all who believe may have eternal life in him.

Commentary: A. Bloom

The Lord himself has taken upon his shoulder the first cross, the heaviest, most appalling cross, but after him thousands and thousands of men, women, and children have taken upon themselves their own crosses, lesser crosses, but how often these crosses, which are lesser than Christ's, remain so frightening for us. Innumerable crowds of people have lovingly, obediently, walked in the footsteps of Christ, treading the long tragic way which is shown by our Lord, a way tragic but which leads from this earth to the very throne of God, into the kingdom of God. They walk, carrying their crosses, they walk now for two thousand years, those who believe in Christ. They walk on, following him, crowd after crowd, and on the way we see crosses, innumerable crosses, on which are crucified the disciples of Christ.

Crosses, one cross after the other, and however far we look, it is crosses and crosses again. We see the bodies of the martyrs, we see the heroes of the spirit, we see monks and nuns, we see priests and pastors, but many, many more people do we see, ordinary, simple, humble people of God who have willingly taken upon themselves the cross of Christ. There is no end to this procession. They walk throughout the centuries knowing that Christ has foretold us that they will have sorrow on this earth, but that the kingdom of God is theirs.

They walk with the heavy cross, rejected, hated, because of truth, because of the name of Christ. They walk, they walk, these pure victims of God, the old and young, children and grown-ups.

150

But where are we? Are we going to stand and look; to see this long procession, this throng of people with shining eyes, with hope unquenched, with unfaltering love, with incredible joy in their hearts, pass us by? Shall we not join them, this eternally moving crowd, that is marked as a crowd of victims, but also as little children of the kingdom? Are we not going to take up our cross and follow Christ? Christ has commanded us to follow him. He has invited us to the banquet of his kingdom, and he is at the head of the procession. Nay, he is together with each of those who walk. Is this a nightmare? How can blood and flesh endure this tragedy, the sight of all these martyrs, new and old? Because Christ is risen, because we do not see in the Lord who walks ahead of us the defeated prophet of Galilee as he was seen by his tormentors, his persecutors. We know him now in the glory of the resurrection. We know that every word of his is true. We know that the kingdom of God is ours if we simply follow him.

(*Meditations — A Spiritual Journey*, 123-125)

Anthony Bloom (1914-), Metropolitan of Sourozh, born Andre Borisovich Bloom in Lausanne, Switzerland, was educated at the Sorbonne, became a doctor of medicine before taking monastic vows in 1943 and became a priest of the Russian Orthodox Church in Paris in 1948. In 1960 he was ordained archbishop of Sourozh and then became in 1965 Metropolitan and Patriarch of Moscow and All Russia in Western Europe. He lectured in various parts of the world and authored many books on prayer and the spiritual life.

All Saints

Gospel: Matthew 5:1-12

When Jesus saw the crowds he went up on the mountainside. After he had sat down his disciples gathered around him, and he began to teach them: "Blessed are the poor in spirit; the reign of God is theirs."

Commentary: K. Adam

Hosts of the redeemed are continually passing into heaven, either directly or by the road of purification in the suffering Church. They pass into the presence of the Lamb and of him who sits upon the throne, in order face to face—and no longer in mere similitude and image—to contemplate the Trinity, in whose bosom are all possibilities and all realities, the unborn God from out of whose eternal well-spring of life all beings drink existence and strength, motion and beauty, truth and love. There is none there who has not been brought home by God's mercy alone. All are redeemed, from the highest seraph to the new-born child just sealed by the grace of baptism as it left the world. Delivered from all selfish limitations and raised above all earthly anxieties, they live, within that sphere of love which their life on earth has traced out for them, the great life of God. It is true life, no idle stagnation, but a continual activity of sense and mind and will. It is true that they can merit no longer, nor bear fruit now for the kingdom of heaven. For the kingdom of heaven is established and grace has finished its work. But the life of glory is far richer than the life of grace. The infinite spaces of the being of God, in all its width and depth, provide a source in which the soul seeks and finds the satisfaction of its most intimate yearnings. New possibilities continually reveal themselves, new vistas of truth, new springs of joy. Being incorporated in the most sacred humanity of Jesus, the soul is joined in most mysterious intimacy to the Godhead itself. It hears the heartbeats of God and feels the deep life that pulsates within the Divinity. The soul is set and lives at the center of all being, whence the sources of all life flow, where the meaning of all existence shines forth in the triune God, where all power and all beauty, all peace and all blessedness, are become pure actuality and purest present, are made an eternal now.

This life of the saints, in its superabundant and inexhaustible fruitfulness, is at the same time a life of the richest variety and fullness. The one Spirit of Jesus, their head and mediator, is manifested in his saints in all the rich variety of their individual lives, and according to the various measures in which every single soul, with its own special gifts and its own special call, has received and employed the grace of God. The one conception of the saint, of the servant of Christ, is embodied in an infinite variety of forms. The litany of the saints takes us rapidly through this "celestial hierarchy." And while every name denotes a special gift, a special character, a special life, yet all are united in one only love and in one gospel of joy and gladness.

(*The Spirit of Catholicism*, 120-122)

Karl Adam (1876-1966) was born in Bavaria, studied for the priesthood and was ordained in 1900. After some experience of pastoral work he taught first at the University of Munich and in 1918 became a professor at Strasbourg. A year later he was appointed to the chair of dogmatic theology at Tübingen, which he held until 1949. He was among the forerunners of ecumenism, liberal and up to date in thought, but always orthodox. His writings, which had great influence especially on the laity, include: *The Spirit of Catholicism, Christ Our Brother,* and *The Son of God.*

All Souls

Gospel: Luke 7:11-17   Young man, I say to you, arise.

Commentary: Catherine of Genoa

There is no joy save that in paradise
to be compared with the joy of the souls in purgatory.
As the rust of sin is consumed
the soul is more and more open to God's love.
Just as a covered object left out in the sun
cannot be penetrated by the sun's rays,
in the same way,
once the covering of the soul is removed,
the soul opens itself fully to the rays of the sun.
Having become one with God's will,
these souls, to the extent that he grants it to them,
see into God.
Joy in God, oneness with him, is the end of these souls,
an instinct implanted in them at their creation.
All that I have said
is as nothing compared to what I feel within,
the witnessed correspondence of love
between God and the soul;
for when God sees the soul pure as it was in its origins,
he tugs at it with a glance,
draws it and binds it to himself with a fiery love.
God so transforms the soul in himself
that it knows nothing other than God.
He will not cease
until he has brought the soul to its perfection.
That is why the soul seeks to cast off
any and all impediments, so that it can be lifted up to God;
and such impediments
are the cause of the suffering of the souls in purgatory.
Not that the souls dwell on their suffering;

they dwell rather on the resistance they feel in themselves
against the will of God,
against his intense and pure love bent on nothing
but draw them up to him.
And I see rays of lightning
darting from that divine love to the creature,
so intense and fiery as to annihilate not the body alone
but, were it possible, the soul.
The soul becomes like gold
that becomes purer as it is fired,
all dross being cast out.
The last stage of love
is that which does its work without human doing.
If humans were to be aware
of the many hidden flaws in them
they would despair.
These flaws are burned away in the last stage of love.
God then shows the soul its weakness,
so that the soul may see the workings of God.
If we are to become perfect,
change must be brought about in us and without us;
that is, the change is to be the work not of human beings but of God.
This, the last stage of love,
is the pure and intense love of God alone.
The overwhelming love of God
gives the soul a joy beyond words.
In purgatory great joy and great suffering
do not exclude one another.

(Purgation and Purgatory, 71-82)

Catherine of Genoa (1447-1510) was married at the age of sixteen to Giuliano
Adorno. After ten unhappy years she was suddenly converted to ardent love of
God. Later her husband too was converted and helped her to care for the sick
in a hospital at Genoa. Her teachings, compiled by others, are contained in
Purgation and Purgatory and *The Spiritual Dialogue*.

Dedication
of the Lateran Basilica

Gospel: Luke 19:1-10

Entering Jericho, Jesus passed through the city. There was a man there named Zacchaeus, the chief tax collector and a wealthy man. He was trying to see what Jesus was like, but being small of stature, was unable to do so because of the crowd.

Commentary: H. de Lubac

The mystery of the Church is our own mystery par excellence, for it is in his Church that God looks upon us and loves us, in her that he desires us and we encounter him, and in her that we cleave to him and are made blessed. She is the mountain visible from afar, the radiant city, the light set on a candlestick to illuminate the whole house. She is the "continual miracle" which is always announcing to people the coming of their Savior and manifesting his liberating power in examples without number; she is the magnificent vaulting under which the saints, like so many stars, sing together of the glory of the redeemer.

To a person who lives in her mystery she is always the city of precious stones, the heavenly Jerusalem, the bride of the Lamb, as she was to Saint John; and seeing her thus, he feels that very joy which bursts through the light-split skies of the Apocalypse and glows in its serene visions. One begins to understand what made Saint Augustine cry: "When I talk about her, I cannot stop."

Saint Clement of Alexandria said superbly, "Just as the will of God is an act, and is called the world, so also his intention is the salvation of all people, and is called the Church." So we should say of the Church, as of Christ, that her kingdom *shall be without end*, for the *nuptials of the Lamb* are eternal. For the elect salvation consists in being welcomed into the heart of the Church for which they were created, in which they have been predestined and are loved.

Holy Church has two lives, one in time and the other in eternity. We must always keep a firm hold on the continuity of the one Church through the diversity of her successive states. Prior to the incarnation, before she had become the bride, she was the betrothed only; and that remains true to a certain extent until the end of time, in that the mystical marriage of Nazareth and Calvary needs the final parousia as its fulfillment. All the same, the Church has already received an incomparable betrothal gift, since her bridegroom has given her his very blood.

It is one and the same Church that is to see God face to face, bathed in his glory, and yet is our actual Church, progressing laboriously in our world, militant and on pilgrimage, humiliated daily in a hundred ways. In the depths of her being she is already the city of God; through the virtue of faith she has already been brought into the storerooms of the king. This holy Jerusalem is, mysteriously and in hope, the heavenly Jerusalem; our earthly mother is already our heavenly mother, and the doors which she opens to us are already the heavenly gates. There will be yet one more changing of brass into gold and iron into silver; but in and through this future transmutation she will always be "the same city of Yahweh, the Zion of holy Israel": "This is heavenly and that is heavenly; this is Jerusalem and that is Jerusalem." We ought, indeed, to love that very element in the Church which is transitory, but we ought to love it as the one and only means, the indispensable organ, the providential instrument; and at the same time as the pledge, the passing image, the promise of the communion to come.

(*The Splendor of the Church,* 25-54, passim)

Henri de Lubac (1886-1991), after the study of law, entered the Society of Jesus in 1913 at Saint Leonary in Great Britain and taught fundamental theology at the Catholic Faculty of Lyon. With Cardinal Daniélou he founded in 1940 the series *Sources Chrétiennes*. From 1960 onward he was a member of various Vatican commissions in preparation for the Council, and after the Council continued to work on various commissions. He was created a cardinal by Pope John Paul II in 1983. He authored numerous books and articles, his book *Catholicism* being his masterpiece. Cardinal de Lubac died in 1991.

Immaculate Conception

Gospel: Luke 1:26-38

The angel Gabriel was sent from God to a town of Galilee named Nazareth, to a virgin betrothed to a man named Joseph, of the house of David. The virgin's name was Mary. Upon arriving, the angel said to her: "Rejoice, O highly favored daughter, the Lord is with you. Blessed are you among women."

Commentary: R. Knox

The feast of our Lady's Immaculate Conception, which we celebrate today, is the promise and the earnest of Christmas; our salvation is already in the bud. As the first green shoot heralds the approach of spring, in a world that is frost-bound and seems dead, so in a world of great sinfulness and of utter despair that spotless conception heralds the restoration of man's innocence. As the shoot gives unfailing promise of the flower which is to spring from it, this conception gives unfailing promise of the virgin birth. Life had come into the world again, supernatural life, not of man's choosing or of man's fashioning. And it grew there unmarked by human eyes; no angels sang over the hills to celebrate it, no shepherds left their flocks to come and see; no wise men were beckoned by the stars to witness that prodigy. And yet the first Advent had begun. Our Lady, you see, is the consummation of the Old Testament; with her, the cycle of history begins anew. When God created the first Adam, he made his preparations beforehand; he fashioned a paradise ready for him to dwell in. And when he restored our nature in the second Adam, once more there was a preparation to be made beforehand. He fashioned a paradise for the second Adam to dwell in, and that paradise was the body and soul of our blessed Lady, immune from the taint of sin, Adam's curse. It was winter still in all the world around; but in the quiet home where Saint Anne gave birth to her daughter, spring had begun.

Man's winter, God's spring; the living branch growing from the dead root; for that, year by year, we Christians give thanks to God when Advent comes round. It is something that has happened once for all; we look for no further redemption, no fresh revelation, however many centuries are to roll over this earth before the skies crack above us and our Lord comes in judgment. Yet there are times in history when the same mood comes upon us, even upon us Christians; the same mood of despair in which the world, Jewish and heathen, was sunk at the time when Jesus Christ was born. There are times when the old landmarks seem obliterated, and the old certainties by which we live have deserted us; the world seems to have exhausted itself, and has no vigor left to face its future; the only forces which seem to possess any energy are those which make for disruption and decay. The world's winter, and it is always followed by God's spring.

Behold, I make all things new, said our Lord to the saint of the Apocalypse; let us rejoice, on this feast of the Immaculate Conception, in the proof and pledge he has given us of that inexhaustible fecundity which belongs only to his grace. And let us ask our blessed Lady to win for us, in our own lives, that continual renewal of strength and holiness which befits our supernatural destiny. Fresh graces, not soiled by the memory of past failure; fresh enterprise, to meet the conditions of a changing world; fresh hope, to carry our burdens beyond the shifting scene of this present world into the changeless repose of eternity.

(*University and Plain Sermons,* 402-405)

Ronald Knox (1881-1951), son of E. A. Knox, one-time bishop of Manchester, England, was educated at Eton and Oxford. Already noted for the brilliance of his mind, he was appointed chaplain of Trinity College, Oxford, and became a leading figure among Anglo-Catholics. In 1917 he was received into the Roman Catholic Church and ordained two years later. He taught for a time at Saint Edmund's Ware and was chaplain to the Catholic undergraduates at Oxford from 1936-1939. At the request of the hierarchy he then devoted himself to making a new English translation of the entire bible. The New Testament was first published in 1945 and the Old in 1949. As a writer on a wide range of subjects, Knox's thought is often strikingly original and his style characterized by wit.

Acknowledgments

In an anthology of readings it is sometimes difficult to locate all the copyright holders of the individual readings selected. Over the years the copyright holder may have transferred the rights to another company, or the copyright has reverted to another entity. Also there are changes of address, for several requests have been returned.

If I have failed to acknowledge a copyright, please bring it to my attention, and a correction will take place.

When copyright has expired or when a text is translated from the original language, no copyright is mentioned. Thank you.

Anthony Bloom, *Mediations-A Spiritual Journey* (Denville: Dimension Books, 1971).

Pierre Bernard, O.P., *The Mystery of Jesus*, ©1966 Alba House.

Joseph Bonsirven, S.J., *The Theology of the New Testament* (Wellwood, England: Search Press, Ltd-Burns and Oates, Ltd.).

Ladislaus Boros, *God Is With Us*, ©1967 Burns and Oates, Ltd.

Rita Burrows, *To Believe in Jesus*, ©1978 Rita Burrows, Sheed and Ward (London).

Catherine of Genoa, *Purgation and Purgatory, The Spiritual Dialogue*, translated by Serge Hughes, ©1979 by the Missionary Society of Saint Paul the Apostle in the State of New York. Used by permission of Paulist Press.

Teilhard de Chardin, *Le Milieu Divin*, ©1960 Harper and Rowe.

Jean Corbon, *The Wellspring of Worship*, translated by Matthew O'Connell. English translation ©1988 by the Missionary Society of Saint Paul the Apostle in the State of New York. Used by permission of Paulist Press.

Jean Daniélou, S.J., *Le mystère de l'Avent*, ©Editions du Seuil (reprinted by permission of Georges Borchardt, Inc.).

Demetrius Dumm, *Flowers in the Desert, A Spirituality of the Bible*, ©1987 Paulist Press. Used by permission of Paulist Press.

Wilfrid Harrington, *Key to the Bible, Saint Mark*, ©1975 Alba House.

Frances Caryll Houselander, *The Comforting of Christ*, ©1954 Sheed and Ward (London).

Luis de León, O.S.A., *The Names of Christ*, translated by Manuel Durán and William Kluback, ©1984 by Manuel Durán and Michael Kluback. Used by permission of Paulist Press.

Henri du Lubac, S.J., *The Splendor of the Church* (Kansas City: Sheed and Ward).

Hildegard of Bingen, *Scivias*, translated by Mother Columba Hart and Jane
  Bishop, ©1990 Abbey of Regina Laudis: Benedictine Congregation
  Regina Laudis of the Strict Observance, inc. Used by permission of
  Paulist Press.

Johannes Metz, *Poverty of Spirit*, translated by John Drury, ©1968 Paulist
  Press. Used by permission of Paulist Press.

Geoffrey Preston, O.P., *God's Way to Be Human, Meditations on Following
  Christ*, ©1978 English Province of the Order of Preachers. Used by
  permission of Paulist Press.

Karl Rahner, *Biblical Homilies*, translated by Desmond Forristal and Richard
  Strachan, ©1966 Sheed and Ward (London),

Fulton J. Sheen, *The Life of Christ*, ©1958. Reprinted with permission of the
  estate of Fulton Sheen.

Rudolph Schnackenburg, *New Testament for Spiritual Reading*, ©1963 Herder
  and Herder.

Index of Scripture

Index of Authors

Meditations on the Sunday Gospels

JOHN ROTELLE, O.S.A.(ed.)

"*Meditations on the Sunday Gospels, Year A,* is a fine resourse for both preachers and 'ponderers' of the Sunday readings."

Kathleen Hughes, R.S.C.J.
Catholic Theological Union, Chicago, Illinois

"John Rotelle is to be congratulated warmly on this first volume in what will, in time, be an indispensable series on the three-year cycle of the Sunday Gospel."

Dr. Michael Jackson
Christ Anglican Church, Oxford, England

Year A
ISBN 1-56548-032-5
paper, 5 3/8 x 8 1/2, 168 pp., $9.95

Year C
ISBN 1-56548-086-4
paper, 5 3/8 x 8 1/2, 168 pp., $9.95, **Available Fall of 1997**

To order call 1 (800) 462-5980

Journey with the Fathers
Commentaries on the Sunday Gospels

EDITH BARNECUT, O.S.B. (ed.)
Foreword by JOHN E. ROTELLE, O.S.A.

"Each Sunday Gospel is adorned with a reading from one of the early classic writers. The selection is appropriate not only for preparing homilies but also for prayerful meditation."

The Bible Today

"Special care has been taken in making the translations so they may be proclaimed effectively. There is a brief introduction to the life and ministry of each author included in the collection."

Worship

Year A
ISBN 1-56548-013-9, **2d printing**
paper, 5 3/8 x 8 1/2, 168 pp., $9.95

Year B
ISBN 1-56548-056-2, **2d printing**
paper, 5 3/8 x 8 1/2, 160 pp., $9.95

Year C
ISBN 1-56548-064-3, **2d printing**
paper, 5 3/8 x 8 1/2, 160 pp., $9.95

To order call 1 (800) 462-5980